W9-AXF-365

THOSE WERE THE NIGHTS

Photo: copied by Howard M. King

Irving as "Jingle"

THOSE WERE THE NIGHTS

by

JAMES AGATE

With Forty-one illustrations

BENJAMIN BLOM  New York/London

The dramatic performance is given once and for all; it is never precisely repeated; and nothing my dear jewel of a colleague can say will bring back Irving in *The Bells.*

DILYS POWELL *in the "Sunday Times"*

First Published 1947
Reissued 1969 by
Benjamin Blom, Inc., Bronx, New York 10452
and 56 Doughty Street, London, W.C. 1

Library of Congress Catalog Card Number 77-91890

Printed in U.S.A. by
NOBLE OFFSET PRINTERS, INC.
NEW YORK 3, N. Y.

CONTENTS

THE LITTLE BOOKS

Was Irving a Tragedian? *page* 9

An Irving Lecture 9

Ellen Terry in *The Amber Heart* 11

Bernhardt in *Théodora* 13

Mary Anderson in *The Winter's Tale* 16

Irving and Coquelin 19

Pygmalion and Galatea 22

Sweet Lavender 24

Richard Mansfield 26

Irving and Ellen Terry in *Macbeth* 28

A Letter from Sarah 31

The Key to Clement Scott 32

A Tilt at Ibsen 34

Scott's Outburst 37

Gilbert Quarrels with Sullivan 39

A Presentation to Mr. Irving 41

A Letter from Oscar Wilde 45

THE ENVELOPES

Opening of Her Majesty's Theatre 49

Forbes-Robertson in *Hamlet* 66

Trelawny of the Wells   *page*   72

George Alexander Tackles Shakespeare   75

Nellie Farren's Benefit   78

Martin-Harvey in *The Only Way*   83

Lydia Thompson's Benefit   87

A Midsummer Night's Dream   93

Enter Henry Ainley   96

Tree, Mrs. Kendal, Ellen Terry   100

Jeanne Granier in *Les Deux Ecoles* and *La Veine*   103

Réjane in a Round of Plays   107

The Marriage of Kitty   118

Crichton in London and Paris   120

Old Heidelberg   125

Letty   128

John Bull's Other Island   131

Peter Pan   133

Sarah's Hamlet   136

Irving's Last Days   140

Ellen Terry's Jubilee   143

ILLUSTRATIONS

Irving as Jingle	*Frontispiece*
Henry Irving	*Between pages* 12–13
Henry Irving	12–13
Ellen Terry	12–13
Ellen Terry	12–13
Ellen Terry	20–21
Sarah Bernhardt	20–21
Sarah Bernhardt in *Phèdre*	28–29
Sarah Bernhardt in *Phèdre*	28–29
Sarah Bernhardt in *L'Aiglon*	28–29
Sarah Bernhardt in *Pelléas et Mélisande*	28–29
Sarah Bernhardt in *Phèdre*	36–37
Sarah Bernhardt	36–37
Mary Anderson in *A Winter's Tale*	44–45
Mary Anderson	44–45
Rose Norreys in *Sweet Lavender*	44–45
Maude Millett in *Sweet Lavender*	44–45
Edward Terry	52–53
Mrs. Patrick Campbell in *The Notorious Mrs. Ebbsmith*	52–53
H. Beerbohm Tree	68–69
H. Beerbohm Tree	68–69

Johnston Forbes-Robertson · · · · · *Between pages* 76–77

George Alexander in *Much Ado About Nothing* · · · 76–77

John Martin-Harvey · · · · · · · · · 76–77

Henry Ainley · · · · · · · · · · · 76–77

Lydia Thompson · · · · · · · · · · 84–85

Nellie Farren · · · · · · · · · · · 84–85

Mrs. Kendal · · · · · · · · · · · 100–101

Mrs. Kendal · · · · · · · · · · · 100–101

Mr. and Mrs. Kendal in *Clancarty* · · · · · 108–109

Réjane · · · · · · · · · · · · · 108–109

Réjane · · · · · · · · · · · · · 108–109

Réjane · · · · · · · · · · · · · 108–109

Marie Tempest in *Dorothy* · · · · · · · 116–117

Charles Wyndham and Mary Moore in *David Garrick* · 116–117

Nina Boucicault in *Peter Pan* · · · · · · 132–133

Hilda Trevelyan in *Peter Pan* · · · · · · 132–133

Cissie Loftus and Hilda Trevelyan in *Peter Pan* · · 140–141

Jeanne Granier in *La Petite Mariée* · · · · · 140–141

Connie Gilchrist · · · · · · · · · · 140–141

Florence St. John · · · · · · · · · · 140–141

PREFACE

This book is not intended to be a history of the Late Victorian or Edwardian Theatre. It is not a history of anything. It consists of extracts from two collections of newspaper cuttings. And that is all this book pretends to be.

Perhaps I may be permitted a word or two about the illustrations. These are mostly from my own private collection, though I have to thank Messrs. Raymond Mander and Joe Mitchenson for one photograph of Henry Irving, two of Ellen Terry, one of Nellie Farren, one of Henry Ainley, and the three *Peter Pan* pictures. It may be of interest to know that the photographs of Irving and Ellen Terry which come second and fourth in this book hung for many years on each side of Irving's make-up table at the Lyceum Theatre. When Irving died they were given by his valet to Lady Martin-Harvey, who gave them to me. There is no reference in the text to Connie Gilchrist or Florence St. John; the pictures are included for the sake of good measure, because their subjects belong to the period, and because they were two pretty ladies.

I wish to express my thanks to all those photographers who have given me permission to reproduce their work, and to offer my apologies to those whose addresses I have not been able to trace.

June 22, 1946   J. A.

NOTE

The articles in the "Little Books" are dated, and the name of the newspaper has been preserved. Wherefore I tender to the proprietors and editors of the *News Chronicle*, the *Daily Telegraph*, the *Evening Standard*, *The Stage* and the *Star* my thanks for their courteous permission to reproduce matter culled from their columns. I have to thank Vyvyan Holland, Esq., for permission to reproduce the letter written by Oscar Wilde to the *Daily Telegraph*, and Messrs. Benn Bros., Ltd. (proprietors of T. Fisher Unwin), from whose publication, *Playhouse Impressions*, the late A. B. Walkley's account of Irving has been taken. In the matter of the "Envelopes" the names of the papers have been deleted by the original collector. While supplying the dates, I have thought it proper to refrain from guesswork ; nevertheless, I tender my acknowledgments in those unidentifiable quarters in which they are due.

INTRODUCTION

The way this book came about is as follows. On a date in 1940, when I was living at Oxford, the post brought me a gift from an anonymous donor. Four little volumes of dramatic criticisms in the London Press covering the years 1885 - 1893. Four volumes bound in some shiny, unidentifiable black stuff, carefully gummed and patched but falling to pieces. To me of enthralling interest, but not quite long enough to make a book. So I put them carefully by. Then, in the month of May, 1946, the postman brought another parcel. This time it was a large one, and being opened it was found to consist of a hundred and odd envelopes containing some fifteen hundred criticisms of the London stage for the period 1897 - 1906. The present volume is a putting together and winnowing of the Little Books and the Envelopes. It is not my collection but another's. Two others, to be exact. It is for readers who would call back yesterday. It is a mansion in which I am no more than the caretaker and the reader's "humble, obliged, obedient servant."

Whose words? Irving's, of course. The words with which he invariably concluded his Saturday-night curtain speech. Now let us have a word or two about this actor who cannot be made to live again. Irving was not a tragedian. He lacked the physique, presence, voice, gait. I doubt very much whether he was even a tragic actor. He eked out tragic rôles with something of himself which was unsurpassable. Ellen Terry writes of the last scene in Wills's *Charles I*: "It was not a man coming on to a stage to meet someone. It was a king going to the scaffold, quietly, unobtrusively, and courageously. However often I played that scene with him, I knew that when he first came on he was not aware of my presence nor of any earthly presence: he seemed to be already in heaven." But even pathos of this order does not make a man a tragedian; perhaps it might be helpful to remember that Wills's play was not a tragedy but a drama. Irving was the most *dramatic* actor I have ever seen. In my view he was the exact counterpart of Frédérick Lemaître. A French writer, one Bournonville, has the following about Lemaître as the gambler in Ducange's *Trente Ans, ou la Vie d'un Joueur*: "In this part he goes through all the stages of the

1

gambling mania, from the victim's twentieth to his fiftieth year; sinks down into poverty and crime, goes about begging, a ragged, crook-backed *lazzarone*, with nothing left of all that he once was— except his expressive eyes. He is given a loaf, and told to cut as much off it as he wants; the first slice he puts into his pocket with a '*pour ma famille*' that sets all hearts a-quiver; but when, later on, after committing a murder, he brings gold home to his wife, and replies to her anxious questioning with: '*Je l'ai trouvé,*' a murmur runs through the audience, as if an abyss had suddenly opened before our eyes." This was the sort of thing Irving did supremely well. I don't understand people who say that Irving was not a comedian. My father saw him both as Robert Macaire and Jingle, and was loud in praise of him in both parts. And surely there is no need to remind any old playgoer of his Mephistopheles? All my memories of Irving are centred not in his overwhelming pathos but in his sardonicism and incredibly sly and subtle sense of fun.

Here I call upon an older and better critic—A. B. Walkley.

To touch the imagination in the playhouse world of Romance and, withal, to bring the great outer Philistine world to its knees—to set our ears ringing with the "chink-chink" of the Polish Jew's sleigh-bells, and to get elected to the Athenæum Club *honoris causâ*—is an achievement verging on the paradoxical; it is running with the hare and hunting with the hounds. Alone among actors, Mr. Irving has taken this double-first: a success on the stage and off it—*in republica tanquam in scena*, as Lord Coleridge once said of him in the words of the great Roman orator. Of his predecessors, Macready came near doing it, but failed. For Macready was a bit of a Philistine—was, in fact, among the drabs. He was ashamed of his profession. Mr. Irving is proud of it, feeling a stain on its honour "like a wound." Burke's phrase comes naturally to the mind, for there is something chivalric in the man as in the player—a dignity, a gusto, a touch of the hidalgo. When a quarter of a century ago Henry Irving, after ten years' rustication, was permanently enrolled in a London company, the prospects of the English stage were, as Mr. Stevenson would say, aleatory. The die might have come down drab; our next great actor might have been a John Kemble or an elder Farren, a classic, a depositary of "correctness" and the traditions. Like every other young actor, Irving began by doing what Théodora, in Sardou's play, says her imperial husband does—*un peu de tout*. Of these miscellaneous experiments, our elders still profess to remember with gratitude the actor's Richard

Chevenix, his Rawdon Scudamore, his Jeremy Diddler, his Bill Sikes. He was by no means an ideal Claude Melnotte. Then he fell to playing Doricourt, Charles Surface, Young Marlow, Captain Absolute, drab heroes to a man. But this was only a trial of the die; the gambler's first throw "for love." When it was finally cast, it came down flamboyant. The actor approached his proper goal of the romantic, the fantastic, in Digby Grant, in Jingle, and reached it, amid a roar of astonished applause from the crowd, in Burgomaster Mathias. This was his first great assault on Philistia. It roused the average sensual man to the disquieting consciousness of a nervous system. Contrast it with M. Coquelin's impersonation of the same part, and you have the pass-key to Mr. Irving's method. The one is of imagination all compact, a common Alsatian innkeeper transfigured by romance, seen, as it were, by flashes of lightning; the other is plausible, logical, correct; a figure of cold daylight, leaving you as cold. In a word, the one is flamboyant; the other only drab.

It was evident from the first that he had not the fluid or ductile temperament which makes your all-round actor, your Betterton, your Garrick. His mind was not like Squire Brooke's, a jelly which ran easily into any mould. Here, again, his method is antithetic to M. Coquelin's. Universality is the foible of M. Coquelin, who—in defiance of a nose suggesting obvious limitations—thinks with Colley Cibber that "anything naturally written ought to be in everyone's way that pretends to be an actor." Mr. Irving's individuality is too strongly marked to let him fall into that heresy. As soon as he attacked Shakespeare we saw that he was not going to sweep the board. He began—of course, they all do—with Hamlet. It is a part in which no actor has ever been known entirely to fail; but it will never be linked with Mr. Irving's name as it is, for all time, with Betterton's—the classic impersonation, "the best part, I believe," says Pepys, "that ever man acted." His Othello, his Richard, were only half-successes. One still prefers to read how Edmund Kean did them. Over the recollection of his Romeo one passes hastily, suppressing a chuckle. His Macbeth, even in its second version, revised and improved, was rather romantic than tragic. So it was in the romantic rather than the tragic repertory of Shakespeare, in the figures painted from the rich fantastic palette of the Italian Renaissance, that one waited for him confidently. Shylock, Iago, Malvolio, Benedick, these are all flamboyant parts, and he took possession of them by right of temperament. To say that his "was the Jew that Shakespeare drew" would be to quote Pope's doggerel inopportunely. It was the Jew idealised in the light of the modern Occidental reaction against the *Judenhetze*, a Jew already conscious of the Spinozas, the Sidonias, the Disraelis, who were to issue from his loins. His Iago was daringly Italian, a true compatriot of the Borgias, or rather better than Italian, that "devil incarnate, an Englishman Italianate." The remembrance of those grapes which he plucked and slowly ate still sets the teeth of Philistia on edge. His Malvolio had an air of *hidalguia*, something of Castilian loftiness, for all the fantasy of its cross-gartering; Don Quixote turned Major Domo. Quite the best of his Renaissance flamboyants is his Benedick, as gallant a picture of the courtier-scholar-soldier as anything in the pages of Cellini, or the canvases of Velasquez. But, grateful as we are for these things, his greatest services to Shakespeare, most of us will think, have been less immediate than mediate, less as actor than as manager. Nero did not surpass, nor the late M. Perrin equal, him as a *metteur-en-scène*. His series of Shakespearean land- and sea-scapes, Veronese gardens open to the moonlight, a Venice unpolluted by Cook's touristry, groves of cedar and cypress in Messina, Illyrian shores, Scotch hillsides, and grim castles, Bosworth Field—what a panorama he has given us! The sensuous, plastic, pictorial side of Shakespeare had never been seen before he showed it. Here you have the flamboyant artist outdoing Delacroix on his own ground.

Nevertheless, man cannot live by Shakespeare alone, least of all this man. His most permanent triumph has been in melodrama—which is Philistia's name for the stage-flamboyant expressed in prose. His prototype in this was Lemaître; and his conquest of the Lemaîtrist repertory is complete. His Robert Macaire, his Dubosc, are the most effective of stage sudorifics. French melodramas, too, have yielded him Louis XI, the two Dei Franchi, while two of Macready's great parts—played in a manner widely different from Macready's—have furnished him with Richelieu and Werner. These are all studies in the lurid, the volcanic, and they are among his strongest; but two at least of his best things are figures of repose, if not of still life—his Charles I and his Dr. Primrose. Over them all, the just and the unjust, his romance has gleamed impartially.

But, as Sainte-Beuve somewhere says, *L'écueil particulier du genre romanesque, c'est le faux*, and this romantic actor could not hope to escape the special danger of his temperament. Like the Don Quixote with whom I have compared him, he has now and then mistaken spavined hacks for Rosinantes and flocks of sheep for armies. His Vanderdecken, his Eugene Aram, perhaps his Philip, and his Count Tristan, were among these errors. His Mephistopheles, too, and, as some think, his Edgar of Ravenswood. The fault was not all his own. His authors played him false. There one touches him between the joints of his harness; he has failed to create a great modern playwright. Let him crown his career by doing that, and I, for one, will vote for his canonisation. Where is he to find the playwright? Well, at the risk of passing for a Curious Impertinent, I will hint that a great artist in fiction is to be found under the shadow of a certain hill in Surrey. Only to think what the creator of those princely flamboyants, Old Mel and Richmond Roy, might have done—might, surely, still do—for Henry Irving! As George Tesman says, "Fancy that!"

And now to my more immediate object—the cuttings.

The Little Books

WAS IRVING A TRAGEDIAN?

T H E S E begin with H.I.

Mr. Irving has always been a remarkable personality. As an invoice clerk in the office of Thacker and Co. in Newgate Street, he impressed his fellow employees no less by his gentlemanliness and amiability and his conscientiousness in work than by the sense of refinement which prompted him to institute among those who shared his desk a little code of rules by which each agreed to be subject to a small fine for any disregard of the niceties of grammar or the other proprieties of speech.

AN IRVING LECTURE

But at the moment Irving is lecturing or, rather, reading to the Birkbeck Institute, and on *Hamlet*:

D A I L Y N E W S , 24*th February*, 1887

Mr. Irving came upon the stage punctually at eight o'clock with a small, red-bound volume of the play in his hand. This he placed upon a reading-desk, and occasionally referred to it, more by way of form than from necessity, as the whole play, or such part of it as time sufficed to give, was practically recited from memory. It was originally announced that the reading would occupy two hours, but when the second part, which embraced the first three acts, came to an end, Mr. Irving decided to leave out the fourth act altogether and to compress the fifth. Even with these excisions the reading occupied three hours, with the exception of a few minutes' interval, and during the whole of this arduous task the great actor's voice never once faltered or failed, nor did lack of memory ever cause a moment's hesitation. That the physical effort was a great and trying one was evident enough. At the same time, everything that could assist Mr. Irving was at his service. He had an appreciative and an intelligent audience, who did not embarrass him by applause at the wrong time,

9

but were unstinting in their praise when he had concluded the several portions of his task. After the demonstration that greeted his entrance upon the stage a silence that was absolutely perfect succeeded, and was maintained throughout, so that not a word of the tragedy was lost. It is not necessary, after the exhaustive and elaborate criticisms that have appeared of Mr. Irving's rendering of Hamlet, to say anything about it here beyond this, that it stood out distinctly from all the other characters, and a very moderate acquaintance with the dialogue would have been sufficient to let the listener know when the Prince was on the stage. Mr. Irving, with a few rare exceptions, did not introduce his characters by name, and a somewhat marked habit of running sentences uttered by different persons one upon another without pause or inflexion of voice rendered the task of distinguishing between other personages in the play less easy. With the talented exponent of Ophelia sitting before him as one of the audience, Mr. Irving apparently did not think it necessary to read any of the part except the scene with Hamlet in the third act, and the fourth act, as we have said, with Ophelia's mad scene, was omitted altogether. An agreeable relief from the prevalent sombreness of the tragedy was afforded by Mr. Irving's admirable rendering of the colloquy of the gravediggers in the fifth act. Here his powers of comedy were displayed in brilliant contrast to the gloomy and cynical aspect he was compelled to adopt in previous passages. The final words of the dying Prince were uttered with most moving pathos, and it was not until the last syllable had fallen on the ears of the audience, that their concentrated attention was released.

ELLEN TERRY IN *THE AMBER HEART*

It is fitting that the next cutting should be about Ellen Terry. The play was *The Amber Heart*, written by Alfred Calmour, W. G. Wills's secretary. Nonsense which actually saw the footlights, this being Ellen Terry's way of amusing herself while Irving was playing about with *Werner*. This fantasy about what Mrs. Gummidge must have been like at seventeen is full of delightful, unconscious nonsense. Nothing wrong about

> *The land, the sea, the boundless arch of blue*

if it had not been followed by

> *Which makes men giddy when they think of it.*

Again

> *A dead man's neither fish, nor flesh, nor fowl,*

might pass for philosophy but for the succeeding

> *Why, an old rooster is indeed more prized.*

The play was produced on 7th June, 1887, and next morning Clement Scott came out with his usual column. He began:

It was not the memory of Undine, or Beatrice, or Elaine, or Vivien; it was not after reading Fouquée, or Dante, or Tennyson; it was not after diving deep into mediæval romance or modern poetry, that Mr. Alfred C. Calmour sat down to write his pretty story of *The Amber Heart*. It must have been after studying very closely that curious compound of childlike innocence and womanly tenderness, that strange amalgam of German mysticism and Italian fervour, the elf-like weirdness and picturesque idiosyncrasy of the one actress of our time who yesterday secured her surest acting triumph.

Fiddlesticks ! Ellaline at her first appearance says,

> *"When I was born, the fairy bloom was spread*
> *O'er wood and meadow, and the sunny beams*
> *Danced in the shadows to the hedge-bird's song."*

Can that have waked no echo? Or did Scott, snookering himself with Dante, forget that other Beatrice? And where, pray, did he think that Calmour got Coranto's

Stand but upon the summit of a cliff,
And mark what pigmies men and women look
Upon the beach a hundred yards beneath.

The cast included Willard, Kemble, and young Beerbohm Tree, and the play was a success. But the ungammonable leading lady knew the play was rubbish and years later said so.

I remember a supper-party at Courtenay Thorpe's in the 'twenties after which Ellen asked for a cab—not a taxi, but an old-fashioned growler. All muffled up, and with her spectacles on, she said in that voice which was like the heart of a red rose, "Boost me in, Courtenay." And the cabman said, "H'and the lidy as I 'ave the honour of driving h'is Miss h'Ellen Terry. I ain't seen yer, Mum, since you was at the Lyceum in *The Amber 'Eart*—eighty-seven I fink it was." Ellen beamed and, turning to Thorpe, said with a delighted gurgle: "There now, Courtenay, I told you I hadn't altered."

Photo: copied by Howard M. King

Henry Irving

Photo: Lock and Whitfield

Henry Irving

Photo: copied by Howard M. King

Ellen Terry

Photo: copied by Howard M. King

Ellen Terry

BERNHARDT IN *THÉODORA*

And now it is Sarah's turn.

DAILY TELEGRAPH, 19*th July*, 1887

Sarah Bernhardt has returned to us, not as had been expected, tired after her long journey, possibly a little capricious and probably fantastically whimsical, but determined to show that with all her vagaries she can be loyal to her friends when she likes them. She elected to play extremely well last night. She was in the mood. She desired to show us that the golden voice had gained richness and increased melody from her sojourn in the sunny lands of South America; she was nerved at a vital moment of the play to enter with boldness into the domains of tragedy, and with a success that surprised those who have watched her every movement for years past; and all that woman could do to give an electric shock and current to an indifferent play, that Sarah Bernhardt last evening unquestionably did. Sardou's *Théodora* is not a good play—in fact, it is not a play at all: it is a bound-up series of dramatic sketches. It has wonderful moments. The love scene with Andréas, when the guilty Empress hears the song of revolution shouted by the crowd as she is cooing in the arms of the arch conspirator; the murder of Marcellus, whose fate is torture or the declaration of the name of Théodora's lover; the death of Andréas and Théodora—all these are noble scenes, each one of which might make the backbone of a play. But *Théodora* as a whole is fitful and spasmodic, it has fine ideas ignobly carried out, it is a poor specimen of Sardou's skill as a dramatist, and it owes its success wholly to the genius of Sarah Bernhardt. What, then, did she so well last night? What was the scene to which she devoted her best attention? Where was it in the play that she came out and astonished those who are wise, who never express surprise until they really know what this strange being is likely to do? That question is easily answered. It was the murder of Marcellus in which Sarah Bernhardt sounded a note of tragedy last night that was no uncertain one. She had murmured her love speeches love songs we were about to say—in her own incomparable manner; she had curled herself up into wondrous attitudes on the satin couch of reception; she had swayed about in sensual indolence her branch of white lilies, and made the human voice into music as sweet as Nature can give to the voice of woman. Each

13

whisper, each soft murmur of love had been heard distinctly at the
farthest end of the gallery, showing what art and cultivation can do in
these times when they are both so obstinately despised by the ignorant
and the superficial; she had curled in the old fascinating way into the
arms of her lover, saying in tones that can never be forgotten, "*Oh reste!
Oh reste! je te supplie!*" giving to the simple expression "*à ce soir*" a
meaning that only intense expression can give; but, after all, it was in
the murder scene of Marcellus that the great actress surpassed herself.
She is always surpassing herself in certain scenes. Now it is the death scene
of Hernani; now the parting scene in *Fédora;* now the passionate death
farewell of Adrienne, that the actress determines to fix on the memory.
Last night it was that tragic moment when the Empress is left alone with
the man about to be tortured into the betrayal of her lover's name, and
sooner than permit the loved Andréas to be revealed she murders her
friend and conspirator with "a bare bodkin." It was soon seen that the
actress had got a stronger grip of the scene than ever. Her defiant waving
away of the torturers, her insolent defiance of the Emperor Justinian, her
hurried, disjointed, half-incoherent explanation to the bound and wounded
men—were all excellent approaches to the scene. They were the strong
firm chords touched by an accomplished player. But it was when the
wounded Marcellus proposed his own death, and pointed to the stiletto
in the woman's hair, that the audience became astonished into silence.
It was wonderful that so slight and frail a woman could command such
a thrill of excitement. The murder settled and inevitable, the whole face
and physique of the woman seemed to undergo a change. A deadly
pallor spread over the features; the eyes became bloodshot; the hair
hung dishevelled over the brow; the jaw shook nervously; the brand of
Cain was seen on the face of this terror-stricken creature, and she who
but a few minutes before was brightened into beauty with love became
haggard and hideous with crime. At the first plunge the woman's nerve
failed her. The man was too patient, too submissive, too hopelessly at
her mercy. She had not the heart to kill, and in an instant she turned
defeated by the task of slaughter. But when passion stirred her she could
strike, and it was the passionate taunt of Marcellus that nerved this Judith
and laid her innocent victim at her feet. An actress who can excite an
audience to this pitch gets her reward. The reaction comes with a torrent
of applause, and when it is all over the lover of acting in its finest moments
can only regret that Sarah Bernhardt is not always at her best. She has
never in our memory touched that scene as she did last night, in Paris or
in London—not even when the success of the play was at its greatest

height. Luckily for an English audience, the later scenes have been considerably modified and compressed. The scene in the Emperor's study has been omitted, and the death scene of Théodora and Andréas revised and altered. She dies now shrieking out the name of her lover as the fatal cord tightens round her throat.

MARY ANDERSON IN *THE WINTER'S TALE*

After Sarah comes that very different kettle of cold and exquisite fish—Mary Anderson. First something about the play.

DAILY TELEGRAPH, 12*th September*, 1887

Ever since Shakespeare borrowed Robert Greene's *History of Dorastus and Fawnia*, and, scorning geographical accuracy and chronological order, turned it into *The Winter's Tale*, managers have puzzled how to put that play on to the stage in order to make it intelligible to an ordinary audience. The difficulty is not surprising. An author who places Bohemia on the sea-coast, jumps over sixteen years between two acts, begins the action of his story before Perdita is born and ends it when she is ripe for marriage, and alludes incidentally to the Delphic oracle, Christian burial, an Emperor of Russia, and an Italian painter of the sixteenth century, may well puzzle the pedantic manager and the conscientious scene-painter! Garrick in his rough-and-ready fashion did not hesitate what to do. Scorning all sentiment and not caring two straws about Shakespeare's poetry, he cut away the first half of the story altogether, added to the text a preposterous tag for the sake of writing up the parts of Leontes and Hermione, and called this pretty piece of shameless patchwork *Florizel and Perdita*. But they were no respecters of Shakespeare in those days. *The Winter's Tale* was turned into a farce called *The Sheep Shearing*, and both Garrick and Sheridan have written comic songs for Perdita. John Kemble and Macready were not quite so barbarous as Garrick. They had the good taste to restore the story of the jealousy of Leontes, to re-create Hermione; but they could not resist the fascination of Garrick's tag that completely destroyed the dumb mystery and impressive speechlessness of Shakespeare's conclusion. When Hermione is in the arms of Leontes, her forgiven husband, we want no more. The conclusion is there; the story is at an end.

Now about the actress.

Miss Mary Anderson can do nothing that is not interesting to her many admirers. She has been persuaded by some not very judicious friends to double the characters of Hermione and Perdita, which have nothing whatsoever in common. It would be a very wonderful order of mind that in one evening—and for no apparent reason—could plunge from the mental anguish of Hermione, from the seared soul of a tortured and ill-used woman, to the spring-like innocence of a girl sheltered as yet from life's sorrow. The actress, to play Hermione well, to understand Hermione, must put her whole life and soul into the work. Hermione and Perdita are two of Shakespeare's women, two exquisite creations. They are not two pretty figures in a series of *tableaux vivants*. Hermione is more than a beautiful woman posed for a figure on a Wedgwood plaque; Perdita is much more than an artist's model. In seeking change the actress arrived at an even, well-ordered, blameless monotony. The audience did not carry away any idea of wife or daughter, save that the wife was beautiful and the child pretty. As to the soul of the one or the anticipation of the other, all was intellectually a blank. From her delivery of the text it was not easy to detect if Miss Anderson had studied either woman very much save in externals. It did not very much matter what their minds were about, so long as they looked well and posed well. That was the great point, the posing. There were certainly some very fine pictures that were the result of the study of Hermione. After the declaration of the oracle of Delphi, Hermione had at least one magnificent moment. The crouching at the altar during the thunderstorm, the cowering, hunted, terror-stricken attitude, were excellent preludes to that glare of terror with the averted veil, concluding with the covered face and the tall white figure that falls prone with a crash upon the marble floor. If Hermione could have been as inspired in the trial scene as she was here, if she could express as much with her voice and heart as she can occasionally with her face, then there would be no apathy in her audience or depression in her auditorium. As Hermione she was picturesque, as Perdita she was unquestionably pretty. No need to tell how beautiful she looked in the statue scene, though the pedestal and statue are unreasonably high above the ground, diminishing the effect of the picture. Miss Mary Anderson does not, like Mrs. Charles Kean, stand like a bashful maiden, listening to a favoured suitor, to illustrate the lines of Leontes:

> *Oh! thus she stood,*
> *Even with such life of majesty,*
> *When first I wooed her!*

but, as she did in Galatea, stands a living, breathing statue, well worthy of the enthusiasm of Polixenes:

> *Masterly done!*
> *The very life seems warm upon her lip.*

Emerson has given us a remarkable sentence in connection with **our** understanding of Shakespeare, "A good reader can in a sort nestle into Plato's brain; but not into Shakespeare's. We are still out of doors." This is equally true of some of the most ambitious interpreters of Shakespeare. We see them and listen to them, but we are "still out of doors."

IRVING AND COQUELIN

Back to Irving, whom Coquelin had imprudently challenged with his version of *The Bells*, called *Le Juif Polonais*. Except, of course, that the French piece took the field first.

D A I L Y   T E L E G R A P H ,   *8th November*,   1887

In considering the performance by M. Coquelin of Mathis in *Le Juif Polonais* we must never forget that he is not playing the weird and romantic drama *The Bells*, as Mr. Irving has made us understand it, but is following in the footsteps of M. Talien, who, so far back as June, 1869, drew public attention at the little Cluny Theatre to the dramatic version of the story by MM. Erckmann-Chatrian. The Mathis of this simple Alsatian story, as M. Coquelin understands him, is anything but a picturesque personage. He is a rotund, bright-eyed, commonplace little fellow; a miniature L'Ami Fritz without his polish and deep-seated imagination. It is part of the authors' scheme to present to us a man with two lives; to show us how an ordinary Alsatian innkeeper, affectionate to his family, beloved by his friends, the most respected man in the neighbourhood, can, when alone, be troubled with a disagreeable thing called conscience, and be harassed with the thought of a murder committed by him years before, which very crime, by the acquisition of stolen property, was the foundation-stone of his prosperity. But Erckmann-Chatrian are very particular to insist that from the beginning of the play to the end no one except the audience is to know a word about the guilt of Mathis. We who look on read his mind, watch his apprehension, are witnesses of his dreams and nightmares; but the family of the murderer think to the end that his death has been caused by persisting in drinking too much white wine, and that his last moments have been painless and peaceable. Says the Doctor, when the collapse has come, "*C'est fini! M. le Bourgmestre est mort. Le vin blanc l'a tué.*" Says the faithful son-in-law, "*Quel malheur! un si brave homme!*" Says his oldest friend, with a sign of relief, "*C'est la plus belle mort. On ne souffre pas.*" Anxious to impress these simple truths upon his audience, M. Coquelin seems to us to go out of his way to realise the prosaic old innkeeper at the expense of the picturesqueness of the play. Mr. Irving conceived a man whose nerves

19

were unhinged by the action of awakened conscience; M. Coquelin sketches a cheery little old gentleman, who chuckles to himself that he has hoodwinked his neighbours and cheated the law. All the detail of the home-life of the Alsatian innkeeper is admirably sketched by the French actor; to all outward appearance he is the man he personates; but surely it would have considerably enhanced the interest of the play if, without over-accentuating the well-known dramatic points, he had given colour and added force to his soliloquies and to the celebrated dream scene. The English actor used the story to show us how an evil conscience can unnerve and fret a man; the French actor insists that by an unimaginative mind and unsensitive nature the twinges of uncomfortable recollection can be comparatively ignored. According to M. Coquelin's idea the entrance of Mathis should be undemonstrative and ineffective. It is only a simple old fellow coming home from a fair in Alsatia, so why make a fuss about it? When he tells his family that he has seen a mountebank who sends men to sleep and reads their minds, this uncomfortable fact does not seem to awake the slightest suspicion, or in any way trouble the merry little fellow. His face betrays no sudden flash of recollection. Even when the name of the Polish Jew is mentioned there is only one quick change of expression which is instantaneously followed by a chuckle. The dream bells jingle, but the stolid countenance remains immovable. It is only when the duplicated Polish Jew comes into the inn that Mathis utters one sharp and sudden cry, not of terror but of pain. His friends and the good doctor think it is only an indigestion pang—that he has taken too much white wine. But if the first act, that elsewhere we have found to be so varied, so absorbing, and so full of interest, be comparatively tame and uneventful, what shall be said of the colourlessness of the second?

We say to ourselves, let M. Coquelin only be left alone on the stage, and he will become a totally different man. Not a bit of it. He goes on chuckling with his conscience, not wrestling with it. He hugs himself with delight that there are such fools in the world, but apparently he has no apprehension. The scene with the money-bags, how tame—the discovery of the bit of gold left from the robbery, how it is slurred over! Mathis puts the blood-money into his pocket without so much as a shudder. Who can forget the agonised look of Mr. Irving when he separated the bloodstained coin from the marriage portion? Again, in the scene with Christian, who is getting gradually near the truth, there is no change of expression, nothing to indicate what the old man is thinking of, except that he is a remarkably clever fellow who will hoodwink even the conscientious young officer. In the gay scene of the marriage contract,

Photo: "The Theatre"

Ellen Terry

Sarah Bernhardt

with its old song and dance, there is no attempt to bring Mathis into the front group of the picture. The bells—and dreadfully bad bells they are, by the way—ring in the ears of the burgomaster; but he apparently heeds them not, as he dances behind the stove when the curtain falls upon a succession of scenes pretty enough in their way, but destitute of significance. Necessarily there must be a change in the last act. It is impossible to play the dream scene in the same unimaginative, uneventful fashion. Here M. Coquelin showed some power, but little variety; he was alternately angry and lachrymose; he was savage and weak. He enacted the murder with some attempt at vigorous treatment, but when the curtain fell finally it was felt that, purposely or not, the actor had neglected to observe the psychology of the play, had cast from his consideration all notion of a conscience-haunted man, had refused to unbare his mind even to his audience, but preferred to show us what a somewhat commonplace little Alsatian burgomaster would do if he were suddenly confronted with the recollection of a crime that does not apparently weigh very heavily on such mind as he possesses.

PYGMALION AND GALATEA

Julia Neilson makes her bow, the occasion being a revival of
W. S. Gilbert's *Pygmalion and Galatea*.

DAILY TELEGRAPH, *22nd March*, 1888

There must always be a special interest taken by the intelligent public
in any revival of Mr. W. S. Gilbert's beautiful play *Pygmalion and Galatea*,
particularly when Miss Mary Anderson consents to impersonate the
lovely statue come to life, and to enchant enthusiastic audiences with her
wealth of comedy effects and ideality of attitude. This quaint, half-
imaginative, half-satiric poem was performed yesterday afternoon for
the benefit of Mr. Charles Abud, and it drew a house crowded from
floor to ceiling. Early in the afternoon the Strand was blocked with
carriages in the Lyceum neighbourhood, and it was evident that there
was some very special interest taken in the revival of a familiar work.
Truth to tell, it was not only for the sake of discoursing once more on
Miss Mary Anderson's loveliness and admiring her graceful attitudes; not
only for discussing for the thousandth time how far Mr. Gilbert's curious
conceit approached to poetry or how far fell short of it. There was something else in the wind; there was another surprise in store. It was Miss
Mary Anderson who discovered for herself the value of Mr. Gilbert's
Galatea; it was Mr. Gilbert himself who was said to have discovered a
Cynisca who could rival the Galatea in beauty, equal her in grace, and
follow her when "she put forth the charm of woven paces and of waving
hands." For, as everyone knows, the school of Mary Anderson is that of
wave and curve, of restless movement and of undulating attitude. The
part of Cynisca was chosen for the début of Miss Julia Neilson, why it
would be difficult to say. Cynisca is not a girl. Cynisca is the artistic
balance of Galatea; she is the loving wife, the woman of flesh and blood
and heart and human being, as contrasted with the maiden, innocent,
and visionary Galatea. The curtain had not risen many minutes before it
was discovered that there were two Galateas in the field, but no Cynisca.
In the absence of Miss Anderson, the newcomer, who had so much
intelligence, such pronounced youth, such palpable inexperience, would
naturally be cast for Galatea. Such a part would hide the defects that
unfortunately come prominently into notice in such a character as the

tender-hearted, warm-blooded, and passionate wife. It is as yet premature to criticise Miss Julia Neilson. Nervousness before such a desperately critical audience was of course inevitable, and it was some time before she could get her voice under command or her attitudes into discipline. That Miss Neilson has the material for an actress in her there can be little question. She has stature, a fine stage face, a well-toned voice, and a brain to understand what she is doing. Whether she has heart or any deep feeling, any approach to pathos or sensibility in the higher degree, we shall know by and by, when nervousness has disappeared and practice has done its laudable work. It is a pity, perhaps, that this clever girl has been so early trained in what may be called the floating, waving, billowy school of art. Miss Anderson herself, with her incomparable grace and her extreme skill in posing, often spoils the effect of a speech by her restlessness of limb. She must be for ever stretching out her arms or adjusting her drapery, or bending herself into attitudes, or clinging or clasping, whereas the meaning of the text is often more clearly shown by absolute quiet and repose. Miss Neilson has thus early in her career been unhappily advised to wave and wander. She is perpetually posing; using hands, arms, and shoulders to emphasise every word that she has to utter. Luckily she is a tall and graceful girl, who can bend and move in the accepted serpentine fashion without offence, but it is strange that it should be thought advisable that Cynisca should be not a contrast but an echo of Galatea. Briefly, then, at present Miss Neilson is not Cynisca at all; she is not woman enough, she has not passionate power enough, her love does not glow or burn. She looks and moves and talks more as Pygmalion's elder daughter than his wife. She is no Cynisca, but she is a young, pretty, and very promising Galatea of the future.

SWEET LAVENDER

William Archer, writing of Clement Scott, the famous critic of the *Daily Telegraph*, said: "Mr. Scott represents to a nicety the average middle-class Englishman. He found the stage, in the 'sixties, beneath his intellectual level, and sought to raise it. From 'seventy to 'ninety it exactly came up to his intellectual and artistic requirements, and he was happy. In 'ninety it took a fresh start and left him behind; and he now shrieks to it to come back and 'mark time,' for he cannot follow it into 'an atmosphere that is mephitic.'" Let us see what Scott had to say about *Sweet Lavender*. I cull a fragment from

DAILY TELEGRAPH, *22nd March*, 1888

The best praise that can be given to *Sweet Lavender* is that it is one of those rare and exceptional plays of which, when the curtain has fallen, we somehow feel so little weary that we should like to see it all over again. We have seen far too little of its delightful characters; we leave the play as we close the happy novel with a sense of unfeigned regret. We should like to see more, know more of the pleasant people in whose society we have spent such agreeable hours. We have laughed so heartily that we should like to remember many of the witty things and pregnant sayings that literally set the theatre in a quick spontaneous roar. We have been touched so quickly and so deeply that it seems a shame when the curtain divides us from the homely, honest characters we have learned to love.

Where are they, and why do they disappear and part from us so soon? Brave, generous-hearted Clement Hale, who loved the purity in woman, though he found it and treasured it in the heart of his housekeeper's daughter; poor, mistaken, drink-loving Dick Phenyl, the outcast barrister, who would have fallen into the mire of Fleet Street but for the help of the strong hand of his friend and chum; Ruth Rolt, the silent, grief-enduring housekeeper and laundress, who locks up the secret of her bitter past for the sake of the child she loves, and is enabled to forgive the man who ruined her; fine old manly tender-hearted Geoffrey Wedderburn, who finds in his hour of anguish the help and sustenance of the one woman in the world whose life he has embittered; and fragrant

24

among these weeds and ill-assorted flowers the London child, the sprig of Sweet Lavender, who loves with earnestness, and whose love to her means life or death. Does it not seem churlish to give us these kindly people, and to take them so soon away? But they are only a moiety of the characters that spring from Mr. Pinero's welcome fancy. We have said nothing of the gentle physician who leaves his West End patients to attend the sick and sorry in deserted chambers; or of the cheery bright young American who follows an English girl with persistency until he wins her; or of Mr. Maw, the solicitor; or of Mr. Bulger, the Temple hairdresser; and surely not half enough of Minnie, the delightful English Minnie, who can sympathise with unhappy lovers and resent an insult, brush a carpet, or wash up tea-things, without losing one jot of her dignity or one grain of her self-respect. But where are the villains, where are the adventuresses, where are the men who go off to their doom in handcuffs and the women who are beaten by their husbands on the stage? What contrast is there to the unruffled serenity of this human story? Alas!—let not the realists hear it, whisper it very secretly—but an audience has actually cheered a play as modern plays are seldom cheered, and showered congratulations on an author with very special fervour, because they have actually sat out and enjoyed a piece in which from first to last there is no suggestion of baseness, no atmosphere of evil, no odour of crime. We doubt if anyone present last night regretted or deplored this unfortunate omission on the part of the unobservant author; the laughter that pealed around the house was only occasionally checked by those fits of sudden coughing that denote suppressed emotion; and it is very much to be feared that those who believe that the dawn of the drama will never come until nature has been extracted from it will have to wait until the perfume of *Sweet Lavender* is exhausted, and that—if we may dare to prophesy—will be many a long month hence.

RICHARD MANSFIELD

Mansfield catches it hot.

DAILY TELEGRAPH, *2nd October*, 1888

It is an invidious task to tell unpalatable truths to artists whose ambition is far stronger than their talent, and who are persuaded that clever trick will pass muster for genius; but it is well not to shirk an obvious responsibility. The much-vaunted *Parisian Romance*, that so delighted American audiences, was received last night with the grave solemnity of distrust, and both play and actor were awarded a firm but respectful negative. Mr. Richard Mansfield cannot justly complain of any irritability, prejudice, or ill-treatment. For once in a way the temper of the audience was singularly mild. There were no interruptions, no disturbances, nothing to agitate the nerves of the performers; the play crept on dismally to its dreary conclusion, and when the curtain fell there was a faint summons of courteous recognition before the audience slowly departed in solemn silence. The reason of this was obvious. Octave Feuillet's play, not a good one at the best, requires a style and finish foreign to the nature and capability of Mr. Mansfield's company. Written in pretentious and inflated phraseology, stuffed full of meaningless and inelegant diction, bombastic in tone and wholly vulgar in expression, there was nothing to save such a drama but acting of a high order, and some special sign of talent that would immediately arrest the attention. It was patiently waited for, but it never came. We were introduced to the salons of the highest Parisian society; we were supposed to see the fatal effects of luxury in the most advanced form of modern civilisation; at one time in a fashionable drawing-room, at another in the dressing-room of a Lutetian Sir Harcourt Courtley; now with ladies of title, and now with the choicest specimens of the half-world. The idea was there, but the result was nothing but pretentious feebleness and ambitious incompetence. Much has been said and written of Mr. Mansfield's performance of the Baron Chevrial. We are told that it took New York by storm; but it must have appealed to audiences whose critical judgment was not biased by memories of Robson, or a study of such a modern artist as St. Germain. That Mr. Mansfield is clever no one will deny, but that he has in this character learned the art of concealing his art few will admit.

To succeed with this old *viveur*, this patched and painted monstrosity, who lives the life of a satyr and dies babbling blasphemy, there must be something of genius in the actor. The audience must be conquered by a *tour de force*. St. Germain succeeded in this, but he never showed his method, he never allowed the audience behind the scenes, he did not exhibit that machinery by which he worked his effects. Allowing for this young actor's anxiety and indifferent health, it must be obvious to his sincerest friends that to carry an audience away with you, to startle, to surprise, and to rise to the height of tragedy—for this old demon's death scene is tragedy in its severest form—something more is needed than clever suggestion and intense application. The amateur is prolific in suggestion; it is the artist who can embody. Actors like Mr. Hare, who are past-masters in the art of detail, who are keenly observant, who study tricks of character and eccentricities of manner, have given us scores of instances of senility and selfishness as startling as Mr. Mansfield's Baron Chevrial. But they have not attempted the delineation of incipient paralysis or the grim horror of actual epilepsy. They have drawn the line exactly where they would be likely to fail. "Know yourself" is a maxim that cannot be too constantly dinned into the ears of the ambitious dramatic student. As yet Mr. Mansfield has not had the experience or the practice to master such a character as this old roué. He could play Sir Harcourt Courtley or Beau Farintosh excellently well; but neither of these eccentric old gentlemen have to drop down dead in a fit whilst toasting abandoned women at a fast supper-party.

IRVING AND ELLEN TERRY IN *MACBETH*

Was Irving's Macbeth a failure? *The Stage* cannot find anything better to say of his performance in the revival of 1889 than that "he depicts an indescribable terror that is fascinating by reason of its very repulsiveness." But let us see what Ellen Terry had to say on the subject in her *Memoirs*.

Henry had played Macbeth before at the Lyceum in the days of the Bateman management; he told me that by intuition he had got the right idea of the character, and had since come to know from fresh study that it was *right*. His confidence in the rightness of his conception was not in the least shaken by criticisms of it, and he always maintained that as Macbeth he did his finest work. "And we know when we do our best," he would add. "We are the only people who do know." Perhaps he was right in putting his Macbeth before his Hamlet, yet I think his *performance* of Hamlet was the greater.

His conception of Macbeth, attacked, and even derided, by the critics of 1888, seemed to me then, and seems to me now, as clear as daylight. But the carrying out of the conception was unequal. Henry's imagination was sometimes his worst enemy. It tempted him to try to do more than any actor can do.

One of his greatest moments was in the last act after the battle. He looked like a great famished wolf, weak with the weakness of an exhausted giant, spent with exertions ten times as great as those of giants of coarser fibre, and stouter build.

Of all men else I have avoided thee.

In that line, once more, he suggested, as he only could suggest, the power of fate. He seemed to envisage a power against which no man can fight, to hear the beat of its inexorable wing. For Macbeth then, no hope, no mercy.

Henry's imagination was always stirred by the queer and the uncanny. This was a great advantage in *Macbeth* in which the atmosphere is charged with strange forces. How marvellously he could have played Lady Macbeth in the sleep-walking scene, which ought above all things to be uncanny! I am not surprised that he was dissatisfied with me in this scene. He knew so well how it ought to be done, and I never came near it.

28

Photo: copied by Howard M. King

Sarah Bernhardt in "Phèdre"

Photo: copied by Howard M. King

Sarah Bernhardt in "Phèdre"

Photo: copied by Howard M. King

Sarah Bernhardt in "L'Aiglon"

Photo: copied by Howard M. King

Sarah Bernhardt in "Pelléas et Mélisande"

Of Sargent's portrait of H.I. as Macbeth, Ellen writes:

Everybody hates Sargent's head of Henry. Henry, also. I like it, but
not altogether. I think it perfectly wonderfully painted and like him, only
not at his best by any means. There sat Henry and there by his side the
picture, and I could scarcely tell one from t'other. Henry looked white,
with tired eyes, and holes in his cheeks and bored to death! And there
was the picture with white face, tired eyes, holes in the cheeks and boredom
in every line. Sargent tried to paint his smile and gave it up.

I have the impression that Ellen did not get near any part of Lady M.,
and this is confirmed by:

THE STAGE, *4th January*, 1889

It is difficult to speak of the Lady Macbeth of Miss Terry. So perfect
has she been in everything else at the Lyceum that we are loath to differ
from her admirers upon the merits of a performance that has evidently
been the outcome of great labour and perseverance. Miss Terry has
based her entire reading of the character upon the supposition that
Macbeth is loved by his wife, that all her evil promptings are but the
outcome of her loving thought for his future; and it must be owned that
Miss Terry in following out this theory plays the part in a generally
consistent manner. But the question arises, did such a love exist? There
is no mention of it in the play. Macbeth frequently addresses his wife in
endearing terms: her dialogue, on the other hand, displays no love for
her lord and master. What little affection she may have comes from
ambition, and it is but as ambition's slave that she urges her husband on
to the bitter end—not that he may benefit, but that she may rule. It may
be questioned if a loving, tender wife such as Miss Terry brings before
us could invoke the aid of the spirits to unsex her, to fill her with direst
cruelty, and "stop up the access and passage to remorse." Could such a
woman laugh and jeer at her husband's fears after the murder is done?
Could she take the daggers from his hands and carefully smear the faces
of the grooms with the dripping blood? Miss Terry's performance is
most interesting, graceful, and at times most poetical, but it does not
suggest the author's creation. The sleep-walking scene is full of charm by
reason of Miss Terry's personality. She looks like a beautiful picture, the
conception of a poetic mind. But her pure white clinging garments and
pain-strained face call for admiration rather than pity and awe.

In the meantime here is some chatter about that first-night audience.

The stalls and boxes were crowded with a notable audience—social, artistic, and literary. That section of Society which delights in Lyceum first-nights was represented by Lord and Lady Londesborough, Lady Dorothy Neville, Mr. and Mrs. Edward Lawson, Sir Morell and Lady Mackenzie, Mr. H. L. W. Lawson, M.P., and Mrs. Lawson (accompanied by Mr. E. H. Hulse, M.P., and Mrs. Hulse), and Sir William and Lady Hardman. The Bar sent Mr. Inderwick, Q.C., Mr. Pinches, Mr. C. Mathews (who brought his young wife), and the Hon. Stephen and Mrs. Coleridge. Art made a goodly show. Mr. Keeley Halswelle was there to see the landscapes he did not design; Mr. Boughton, A.R.A., to admire the work of Telbin and Craven, and the groupings of the master; Mr. and Mrs. Val Prinsep evidently to enjoy the play. Mr. Harry Furniss, with his deft pencil, was observed taking furtive notes; while his humorous and genial chief evidently found himself too much engrossed with tragic pictures to discover in them anything but serious inspiration. Mr. F. C. Burnand, as dramatist, editor, and writer of books, had many colleagues and fellow-workers in the stalls. Mr. J. Comyns Carr is here, and Mr. Frederic Hawkins, taking note, no doubt, of the effect of their literary and critical suggestions, the former in an admirable pamphlet, the latter in two excellent *Theatre* articles. Mr. Russell, the accomplished editor of the *Liverpool Daily Post*, the friend of Bright and Gladstone, has come down from the North to assist in the evening's success. He is the author of several scholarly essays on Irving's work—*Hamlet*, *Faust*, etc. Mr. Frank Marshall, the actor's collaborator in a new edition of Shakespeare, sits near his most exacting critic, Mr. Archer, who, unlike Marshall and a few others around him, has not always been an "Irvingite." Mr. Joseph Knight, Mr. Clement Scott, Mr. Nisbet, and other prominent authorities on plays and players are here in force, as are also leading members of the staffs of several American journals. Journalism, in short, seems more than usually to the fore. Mr. Robinson and Mr. Lucy of the *Daily News* have come together; Mr. Morley of the *Pall Mall* is busy with his note-book, and Dr. Russell, "the Pen of the War," looks on free from the cares of the work he did so well in those bygone days, upon which his friend Yates is pondering between the acts. Nor must we forget to mention that other famous "foreign correspondent", Mr. Beatty-Kingston, who recently interviewed the Pope at the Vatican for the *Telegraph*, a feat worthy of himself and his paper.

A LETTER FROM SARAH

A LETTER IN THE "EVENING STANDARD", 11th *July*, 1889

MADAME SARAH BERNHARDT

To the Editor of the "Standard"

SIR, *Our client, Madame Sarah Bernhardt, has sent to us a letter, of which she has requested us to send you a copy. The letter is as follows:*

"Monsieur—Voulez-vous être mon interprète auprès du public Anglais, pour le remercier pour sa courtoisie, pendant la déplorable représentation de Lena? La Compagnie Française a fait un tour de force prodigieux en jouant hier. A sept heures du soir rien n'était prêt pour la représentation qui commençait à huit heures et demi, et durant toute la soirée nous n'étions occupés, les uns et les autres, que de savoir où se trouvaient les portes, les fenêtres, et les accessoires nécessaires à la pièce. C'est dans des vieux décors de La Tosca que nous avons joué la pièce Anglaise. Alors que l'artiste devait entrer à droite il était forcé d'entrer à gauche, la porte de droite n'existant pas. Le jeu de scène était tué, et les artistes surpris perdaient la tête et la mémoire. Les entr'actes duraient trente à trente-cinq minutes, et nous étions tous sur la scène aidant la mise en état pendant que le public trépignait d'impatience.

"Jamais directeur ne s'est moqué de l'art des artistes avec plus d'insolence. Si je relate ces faits au public, c'est que je veux mettre la dignité de la Compagnie Française à l'abri de reproches immérités, et ma réputation d'artiste en dehors de pareils agacements.

"(Signé) SARAH BERNHARDT"

We are, Sir, your obedient servants,

BRANDON AND NICHOLSON

6 Suffolk Street, Pall Mall, S.W., 10th July

THE KEY TO CLEMENT SCOTT

Gradually the interest in Clement Scott warms up. *Why* was he the, in vulgar modern parlance, Big Noise? Indeed, to the majority of the public, the Only Noise.

S T A R , 29*th March*, 1890

It is Mr. Clement Scott's good fortune not to have been too previous. The drama has become an integral part of modern life; thanks to the Bancrofts, to Mr. Irving, and the *Zeitgeist*, society has come back to the playhouse. It was the psychological moment of dramatic criticism—and Mr. Scott grabbed it. Not only did he come at the right time, but he addressed his appeal to the right people. We have heard of poets' poets. Mr. Scott is the actors' critic. Important as he is as a dramatic critic, he is even more important as a critic of histrionics. For him it is not so much the play which is the thing, as the player. Take up the dailies on your breakfast table after a big first-night, skip the political leaders (as all sensible men do) and devour the "notices." In one you shall find deep Shakespearean lore, in another amusing "impression" of the audience, in another a laborious narration of the plot, but for the histrionics of the thing—how this actress managed the big scene and how that actor forgot his lines, how the Nan of Miss Trois-Etoiles compared unfavourably with the Nan of Marie Wilton; where Miss Terry in the *Dead Heart* is superior, or inferior, to Miss Woolgar—for these delights you must needs fall back upon the *D.T.* It is for this reason that the players swear by (when they don't swear at) Mr. Clement Scott, and justly. His case is the very reverse of Hazlitt's—"the players put him out," writes Talfourd. It is the flesh-and-blood element in the piece, I think, which takes Mr. Scott's fancy captive, not the cold literary element. Hence, if you ever discuss a play with an actor (a rash experiment, not to be lightly attempted), you will find he gets his views from what he calls "the paper". Probe further, and you will find that, for him, "the paper" means— *semper et ubique*—Mr. Clement Scott's.

He came at the right time. He appealed to the right people. Add that he brought the right mood. It has the inestimable advantage of being a thoroughly English mood. It has the true English preference for the

comfortable, the conventional, the pleasant, for things "of good report".
In M. Paul Bourget's categories, we should have to rank Mr. Scott
among the moralists, rather than the mere psychologists. In him, behind
the æsthetic appreciation, lurks an ethical judgment. To such Frenchified
theories as that of Art for Art's sake he turns a deaf ear. New theatrical
types may be as new, and as true as you please, but if they are "unpleasant"
they are not for his market. To him the playhouse is not a dissecting-room,
but an apartment in the House Beautiful. This mood you may or may
not approve; but you cannot deny that it is characteristically English.
Again, it is a thoroughly popular mood. *S'il faut opter*, said La Bruyère, *je
veux être peuple*. The quotation has been applied to M. Sarcey; it is
equally applicable to Mr. Scott. There is nothing esoteric about him.
He has "opted" for the popular ticket. Like the people, he is (I use the
term in its worthier sense) a sentimentalist. One feels that his criticisms
are affairs of the heart quite as much as of the head. Indeed, I for one
should not like to say that the emotion does not, in his case, precede
and generate the thought. Certain cynics (not I) call this "gush." Even
if this were true, it would be a small reproach in the country of Dickens.
But it is not true. "Gush" I take, roughly, to be emotion without thought,
and thought is never lacking in this critic's work. Like the people, too,
Mr. Scott has no exorbitant affection for what the three Miss Poles called
the Fine Shades. His criticisms are all of a piece. Capable, as I make no
doubt he is, of subtle analysis, he prefers to sacrifice that to a vigorous
unity of impression. Subtle analysis, he knows, is a half-hearted thing,
and the man in the street has no stomach for it. Accordingly, his criticism
has little ebb and flow; it overwhelms you with a sudden rush and a
roar.

A TILT AT IBSEN

But in the matter of Ibsen and G.B.S. there were other Clements in the field, notably somebody writing in the *Star* and signing himself "Spectator."

STAR, *26th July*, 1890

It requires an immense intellectual effort to understand Ibsen. Witness the unanimity with which the newspapers, on the production of *A Doll's House* at the Novelty, shirked the effort. "No space." "This is not the place to examine." "Full consideration must be reserved for a future occasion," etc., etc.—you know the trick. The Ibsen commentator is even a harder nut to crack. I am told that the St. James's Hall audience [Mr. Shaw had been lecturing] entreated Mr. Shaw to explain his own meaning, and that Mr. Shaw wouldn't, or couldn't. The one obvious thing was that Mr. Shaw was "going for" all sorts and conditions of men, tomahawk in hand. None need be angry with him for that; it has to be done by every man who opens up new intellectual routes. Remember that in the Redskin novel of your youth the Pathfinder was also a Scalphunter. Premising that, if I fail to explain Mr. Shaw here, I am doing no worse than Mr. Shaw himself, I conceive the gist of his theory of Ibsen to be this. Ibsenism is an attack on conventional idealism. What is idealism? A sense of obligation to conform to an abstract conception of absolute fitness of conduct. Example: Let us suppose a community of a thousand persons organised for the perpetuation of the species on the basis of the British family as we know it at present. Say 700 of them (called Philistines by the others) find the British family arrangement quite good enough for them; 299 find it a failure, but must put up with it since they are in a minority. The remaining person recognises the failure, and becomes an Ibsenite. The 299 have not the courage to face the fact that they are failures, and so persuade themselves that the family in the abstract, the ideal family, is a beautiful institution. These are the idealists, and it is these whom Ibsen attacks. . . .

But there is one passage in Mr. Shaw's lecture where, discarding Schopenhauer, and the theory with which he started, he penetrates, as it seems to me, much nearer to the heart of the matter. Ibsen does *not* attack idealism in the abstract, a thing about as feasible as attacking the Equator. "He admits freely that he is an idealist like his fellow-men;

and that all he wants to insist on is the need for constantly renewing our ideals, throwing out the stale as we take in the fresh; recognising that the truth of yesterday is the superstition of to-day, and above all, never indulging in the dream that it is possible to go back to old ideals."

Here, for once, Mr. Shaw lets us touch solid ground. Here we get a sober, guarded statement; helpful, luminous, into the bargain. Helpful, because it drops the ordinary misleading view of Ibsen, a sort of intellectual island in mid-ocean, and defines his position on the mainland of thought; it gives him, to change the metaphor, intellectual ancestry and relations. Ibsen we now see not as an isolated, uncaused, unrelated monster, but as one of a long line of philosophical dramatists, whose "message" to us has been the need of refashioning our moral ideals. We get him brought into line not only, say, with Dumas *fils*, but with Molière and, to go back to the very beginnings of the philosophic drama, with Æschylus. I make no apology for dwelling a moment on this aspect of the matter, for the discovery of the essential identity of the new with the old should always be an agreeable one. It convinces us of the continuity of the race, comforts us with the assurance that men are not, in Burke's phrase, flies of a summer. Consider, then, the Orestean trilogy of Æschylus—hats off, if you please, before a venerable monument, the first great philosophic drama evolved by the Indo-European race. Orestes has put to death his mother, Clytemnestra (in the *Choephori*), because she has (in the *Agamemnon*) murdered his father. For this he is (in the *Eumenides*) pursued by the avenging Furies (symbolising remorse and punishment) who demand, practically, his head on a charger. But he appeals to the Areopagus, presided over by Athene, and retains Apollo as his Sir Charles Russell. The case of the prosecution is that he has broken the old moral code; he is a matricide; he has stifled what they now call at the Ambigu the *voix du sang*. The defence pleads that Orestes obeyed (like Hamlet) his father's ghost, and the Delphic oracle, and public opinion (as represented by the chorus in the *Choephori*). "You pursue me," he says to the Furies, "why did you not pursue my mother?" They answer, "Her victim was not of her own blood." Then Apollo tells them that the marriage bond is closer than the blood tie. In the end, the Areopagite jury is equally divided, and Athene (converted by Sir Charles Russell Apollo) gives her casting vote in favour of the accused. Orestes is not acquitted, but, in formal deference to the old morality, pardoned. But Apollo dismisses the old savage morality (the Furies) with some very plain language. "Out of this! Go to other countries, where heads fall, where justice puts out men's eyes, where the place reeks of torture and torn members, resounds with the shrieks of the stoned and the groans of the crucified!" In other words, "Ta! ta! the old conventional morality!"

What does all this mean? Simply that Æschylus was an Ibsenite some 2,400 years before Ibsen. He says to the Greek public, Renew your ideals. The old Duty, the *lex talionis*, the vendetta, the exaggerated respect for the "blood is thicker than water" theory. These things are worn out. Even the 700 Philistines now believe in the Furies, the 299 who idolise them are idiots. Recognise that the whole ideal is a fraud. Set free the parrot from his cage, let Nora walk out at the front door, give Orestes his pardon. So Molière in, e.g., *Georges Dandin*. The old morality said to the husband, Kill the faithless wife. One not so old said, Beat her. The new morality (new in the seventeenth century) said, Grin and bear it; it doesn't signify. Don't indulge in the dream that it is possible to go back to old ideals. So Dumas *fils* in, e.g., *Denise*. May a gentleman marry a girl already provided (by someone else) with a baby? The old morality— i.e., the current code of kid-glove honour—says, No. The new morality says, By all means if you feel like it, if the will-to-live carries you that way. These illustrations of Ibsenism may obviously be multiplied *ad infinitum*.

Was Shakespeare, then, an Ibsenite? asks some liberal-minded follower of "our only dramatist." I think not. He did not criticise the current ideals; he found them, like the elder Mr. Weller, "all werry capital," and glorified them. Coleridge called this "keeping at all times on the high road of life." See, for instance, *The Taming of the Shrew*, as a view of the Great Woman Question. But there is this to be said: that Shakespeare, if not an Ibsenite, was a Shawite. His great plays are tremendous poems in praise of the will-to-live. He who has not grasped this truth has not seen the true significance of Richard Crookback or of Falstaff or of Audrey and Touchstone.

Photo: copied by Howard M. King

Sarah Bernhardt in "Phèdre"

Photo: copied by Howard M. King

Sarah Bernhardt

SCOTT'S OUTBURST

Clement Scott on Ibsen's *Ghosts?* Well, perhaps a little.

D AILY T ELEGRAPH , 14*th March*, 1891

On the Ibsen stage the nastiness is inferential, not actual. The characters call a spade a spade in a roundabout and circumlocutory fashion. Those who, actuated by curiosity, expected to find a frankness and direct exposition of fact only equalled by the sensation trials by judge and jury at the Cider Cellars in the days of Baron Nicholson, only found a dull, undramatic, verbose, tedious, and utterly uninteresting play. . . .

It is a wretched, deplorable, loathsome history, as all must admit. It might have been a tragedy had it been treated by a man of genius. Handled by an egotist and a bungler, it is only a deplorably dull play. There are ideas in *Ghosts* that would have inspired a tragic poet. They are vulgarised and debased by the suburban Ibsen. You want a Shakespeare, or a Byron, or a Browning to attack the subject-matter of *Ghosts* as it ought to be attacked. It might be a noble theme. Here it is a nasty and a vulgar one.

In addition to Scott's notice the *Daily Telegraph* had a leading article on the subject. I cull:

D AILY T ELEGRAPH , 14*th March*, 1891

Ay! the play performed last night is "simple" enough in plan and purpose, but simple only in the sense of an open drain; of a loathsome sore unbandaged; of a dirty act done publicly; or of a lazar-house with all its doors and windows open. It is no more "Greek," and can no more be called "Greek" for its plainness of speech and candid foulness, than could a dunghill at Delphi, or a madhouse at Mitylene. It is not "artistic" even, in the sense of the anatomical studies of the Great Masters; because they, in carefully drawing the hidden things of life and nature, did it in the single and steadfast worship of Truth and Beauty, the subtle framework and foundation of which they thus reverently endeavoured to seize. . . .

This new favourite of a foolish school, who is to set aside Shakespeare and Sheridan, and to teach the hitherto fairly decent genius of the modern English stage a better and a darker way, seems, to our judgment, to resemble one of his own Norwegian ravens emerging from the rocks with an insatiable appetite for decayed flesh rather than any Æschylus of the North, who dares to drape with tragic splendour the Furies of Orestes, or even any new and dramatic Schopenhauer full of the sadness of human life, and blind to its gladness. Any healthy-minded critic will rise, we think, from the perusal of this so-called "master's" works with the conclusion that Henrik Ibsen of Skien is what Zola would have been without his invention and analysis, Carlyle without his genius and piety, or the "melancholy Jaques" without his culture and wit, if they also had been born of a seafaring family in a poor fishing village upon the Western Fjords. . . .

Realism is one thing, but the nostrils of an audience must not be visibly held before a play can be stamped as true to nature. It is difficult to expose indecorous words—the gross, and almost putrid, indecorum of this play of *Ghosts*. Suffice it to indicate that the central situation is that of a son exposing to a mother—herself, in past days, a would-be adulteress—his inheritance of a loathsome malady from a father whose memory the widow secretly execrates while she publicly honours and consecrates it. If this be Art—which word, be it remembered, is but the abbreviation of the Greek name for what is highest, most excellent, and best—then the masterpieces of English literature must be found in such vagaries as Ben Jonson's *Fleet Ditch Voyage*, Swift's mad scurrility, and Congreve's lewd coarseness. If this be "Greek simplicity", let us be done with Juliet, and Imogen, and Desdemona, and go to the Lock Hospital for the lovers and heroines of our English stage. Even the "Lady of the Camellias"—that hectic harlot—coughed her frail soul away with some external propriety; but Ibsen's patients expectorate, if we may venture to say so, in public, and air on the stage matters that a blind beggar would hide under his patches. In the name of outraged Art let these people— author, actors, and admirers alike—keep to themselves their clinical confessions and scenes which appertain to Mercury rather than the Muse. If their intellectual food be such literary carrion, let them devour it apart; but, in whatever measure they bring their crapulous stuff into the light of day, and within range of the senses of honest and wholesome folk, we trust that public opinion, backed, if necessary, by the law, will in that measure rebuke and restrain the novel and perilous nuisance.

GILBERT QUARRELS WITH SULLIVAN

And now Gilbert and Sullivan are in the thick of their quarrel. A year earlier one had read:

STAR, 14th May

It is quite true about the Gilbert and Sullivan split. The two kings of Barataria are at such odds that they actually do not speak to one another. Of course it was something very serious that caused the split. The names of W. S. Gilbert and Arthur Sullivan have been spoken of in one breath for years. They have been linked together with a closeness that makes the association of Damon and Pythias a mere casual friendship by comparison; that makes the relations of Mr. Marshall to Mr. Snelgrove sink to the level of casual acquaintance. They have been concerned together in one of the most successful enterprises of the time, and hand in hand have reaped honour and fortune. When Gilbert thirsted, Sullivan needed to drink. Sullivan's hunger was appeased if Gilbert ate. In so long and so close an association there must have been many little differences of opinion, perhaps some great ones? Who knows? But at all events, their close friendship has made nothing of them, small or great. It goes without saying that it is something very terrible that has come between them to sever that friendship. It is, indeed. After their long years of fruitful association they have quarrelled

ABOUT A CARPET.

The Gilbert and Sullivan opera business is run on a sharing system. Expenses of every kind are charged against the receipts, and the profit that is left is divided in fixed proportion between the composer (Sir Arthur Sullivan), the author (Mr. W. S. Gilbert), and the manager (Mr. R. D'Oyly Carte). During Mr. Gilbert's recent Indian tour Mr. Carte bought some new carpets that were required for the business. Mr. Gilbert came back from India and objected to the expense. Mr. Carte, as manager, justified the expense. Mr. Gilbert remained furious about it. The result was a great quarrel between Mr. Gilbert and Mr. Carte.

When Mr. W. S. Gilbert does quarrel with anybody they know it. It is a whole quarrel. Ask *Punch*. Mr. Gilbert appealed to Sir Arthur Sullivan, who was equally interested in the matter. Sir Arthur did not want to quarrel with Mr. Carte or anyone else. He declined to quarrel with Mr. Carte. Consequently he got into a quarrel with Mr. Gilbert. And that paltry carpet has completely split up the association. They do not speak to one another. They will never work with one another again.

A PRESENTATION TO MR. IRVING

Nor has the world forgotten Irving. Here is something culled from a daily paper the name of which is missing. The date is 26th November, 1892.

With the exception of a brief stay at the Princess's in 1859 Mr. Irving did not begin his London career, properly speaking, till 1866, when he took up a very varied round of characters, including Doricourt in *The Belle's Stratagem*, Rawdon Scudamore in *Hunted Down*, Harry Dornton in *The Road to Ruin*, Joseph and Charles Surface, Robert Macaire, Petruchio, Young Marlow, John Peerybingle in *Dot*, Chevenix in *Uncle Dick's Darling*, Jingle in *Pickwick*, and notably Digby Grant in *Two Roses*. These, it may be said, ought to have been sufficient, knowing what we do now of his capabilities, to give him easily a place in the front rank of character actors. A good deal of attention he did unquestionably attract, especially by his Digby Grant, but something further was required for the public to proclaim him their prime favourite. The looked-for opportunity came with the production of *The Bells* on 25th November, 1871. At that time the Bateman management of the Lyceum, under which Mr. Irving was playing, was in desperate straits. Something had to be done, but nobody knew what. It was then that Mr. Irving suggested *The Bells*, an adaptation which had come into his hands of a French drama by MM. Erckmann-Chatrian, called *Le Juif Polonais*. There was no literary merit to speak of in this, and the amateur adapter, Mr. Leopold Lewis, who was something in the law, had vainly hawked it about from manager to manager. "Colonel" Bateman had seen it, and disliked it. What was more discouraging still, another version of *Le Juif Polonais* had been tried at another theatre, and had failed miserably. But Mr. Irving saw great possibilities for himself in the character of Mathias, and the piece was accordingly mounted, though not without difficulty, money having to be borrowed for this purpose to the amount of some £300. *The Bells* was the last card of the Bateman management, and played by Mr. Irving it turned up trumps. The grim study of the spectre-haunted Alsatian burgomaster became the talk of the town, and the admiration bestowed upon Mr. Irving's embodiment was unstinted. So reserved an authority as the late Mr. Dutton Cook remarked that acting at once so intelligent and so intense had not been seen on the London stage for many years, that the piece was listened to with the most breathless attention, and that the actor depicted the agonising fear and the passionate despair of his part with real artistic force. In short, Mathias was a revelation. On this very morning 21 years ago—namely, 26th November, 1871—Mr. Irving, like Byron, woke to find himself famous, unless, indeed, he may have felt that fame had come to him on the previous evening in the unbounded applause with which his performance was greeted. The jargon of criticism has it that Mr. Irving's Mathias compelled attention by its "obvious truth to nature." Nothing could be wider of the mark. A realistic burgomaster would have attracted little notice, as the experience of both M. Coquelin and M. Got, who have essayed the part in the original, attests. What manner of man, in truth, would the leading notable of an obscure Alsatian hamlet a hundred years ago have been? Probably an illiterate peasant, a boor, compensating for his lack of education by a deal of native shrewdness and cunning. On such lines Coquelin, and latterly Got, have depicted him—indeed, their authors left them little choice on the point. Mr. Irving's representation of Mathias as a keenly intellectual and introspective man is wholly idealistic. The character impresses us by the glamour of romance and imagination which is thrown around it, and this is wholly of the actor's creating. The combined mental and physical picturesqueness which is Mr. Irving's most marked characteristic, finds here its fullest scope. Mathias has supplanted the Jingles, the Bill Sikeses, the Eugene Arams, the Robert Macaires, and even the Digby Grants of the actor's repertory, because it contains something of all of them. Traces of it might be found in his Macbeth, his Iago, his Hamlet, his Vicar of Wakefield, and even his Lear. It is an epitome of Mr. Irving's genius. For the actor's personality necessarily colours and shapes every impersonation he attempts. The schoolboy (not Macaulay's) was perfectly right from his own point of view when he declared that bread was a better word than the French *pain*, as denoting something to eat, because bread *was* bread. So we may say of Mr. Irving in *The Bells*, that he is not merely good as Mathias but is Mathias himself. *The Bells* not only lifted Mr. Irving into popularity; it has ever since been a successful play, and so it will remain as long as Mr. Irving is here to act it. With him in all probability it will pass away, since neither the action nor the dialogue contains anything of a striking character which Mr. Irving has not put there. Unhappily, the event which brought fortune to the Lyceum was disastrous to poor Leopold

Lewis, who gave up the law in order to live on his fame as a dramatist, but who fell into drink, and eked out a miserable existence until a few years ago, on a pension generously given him by Mr. Irving.

How this anniversary of the production of *The Bells* came to be selected as the occasion of paying a compliment to the Lyceum chief will be sufficiently obvious from what has been said. The most notable play with which he has been identified attained last night its majority. By a happy thought the members of the Lyceum company, who desired to mark this event, and of whom Miss Ellen Terry was the most active, took into their counsels Mr. Onslow Ford, A.R.A., and the resolution was quickly arrived at to present Mr. Irving with a statuette of himself as Mathias. At the same time, it was decided that the utmost secrecy should be observed in the matter, the intention being to place the counterfeit presentment of the conscience-stricken burgomaster in the chief's dressing-room, so that the gift should come upon him as an agreeable surprise, and of course without a preliminary intimation of any kind. To Mr. Onslow Ford, who is one of Mr. Irving's oldest friends, the task of fashioning the statuette was not only a grateful, but a familiar task. The large marble figure of Mr. Irving as Hamlet, now exhibited at the Guildhall, is his work, and thereby hangs a tale. It is no indiscretion to reproduce here the touching words which Mr. Ford employed yesterday to a representative of *The Morning* in connection with this subject:

"Mr. Irving," said the eminent sculptor, "has always been a kind patron to me. Indeed, I attribute not a little of my own good fortune to the start which he gave me when I received his commission for my statue of him as Hamlet. I was then quite a young man, and little known to fame when without a word of discussion as to the price he gave me what I asked, viz., 1,000 guineas. When the statue had been exhibited at the Royal Academy, in 1884, and had been favourably regarded by the public, I asked Mr. Irving what he would wish me to do with it. 'Keep it in your studio,' he said, 'as it may be of assistance to you until you can find some place where the public can appreciate it.' I thought of the Guildhall, and on asking the opinion of the courteous librarian, I was informed that the then Lord Mayor would most willingly accept it on behalf of the Corporation."

Previously to the composition of this statue of "Hamlet," Mr. Ford had done a small work of the same kind. He has also exhibited at the Academy a head of Mr. Irving. Nothing could have been more welcome to him than the opportunity of doing the statuette of Mathias. A difficulty in his way was the secrecy which had to be maintained in the matter, but from his experience in modelling Mr. Irving, and by dint of a little amiable duplicity, he was enabled to carry out his purpose. The sculptor has caught his subject at a happy moment. Mathias is shewn, holding in his hand a bag of his ill-gotten gold, just at the moment when, awe-stricken, he hears the chink, chink, chink of the sledge-bells of the Polish Jew, whose murder he has upon his conscience. Small as it is, no more successful representation of Mr. Irving than this has been given, pictorial or plastic, in point of pose. The statuette bears the following inscription:

LYCEUM THEATRE, 25TH NOVEMBER, 1892

Presented by his comrades of the

LYCEUM THEATRE

On the 21st Anniversary of his First
Appearance in "The Bells"

25th November, 1871
25th November, 1892

At present the work is in clay. By and by it will be cast in bronze, and it is then intended to place in the pedestal a piece of mechanism, which, on a spring being pressed, will reproduce the terrible chink, chink, chink of the accusing bells, thereby 'giving an artistic completeness to the burgomaster's attitude. When Mr. Irving entered his dressing-room last night, after the first act of *King Lear*, the statuette was facing him on a table.

Photo: copied by Howard M. King

Mary Anderson in "A Winter's Tale"

Photo: copied by Howard M. King

Mary Anderson

Photo: Bassano

Rose Norreys in "Sweet Lavender"

Photo: W. and D. Downey

Maude Millett in "Sweet Lavender"

A LETTER FROM OSCAR WILDE

Last, in the Little Books, is a letter written by Oscar Wilde to the Editor of the *Daily Telegraph*.

SIR,

I have just been sent an article that seems to have appeared in your paper some days ago, in which it is stated that, in the course of some remarks addressed to the Playgoers' Club on the occasion of my taking the chair at their last meeting, I laid it down as an axiom that the stage is only "a frame furnished with a set of puppets".

Now it is quite true that I hold that the stage is to a play no more than a picture-frame is to a painting, and that the actable value of a play has nothing whatsoever to do with its value as a work of art. In this century, in England, to take an obvious example, we have had only two great plays—one is Shelley's Cenci, *the other Mr. Swinburne's* Atalanta in Calydon, *and neither of them is in any sense of the word an actable play. Indeed, the mere suggestion that stage presentation is any test of a work of art is quite ridiculous. In the production of Browning's plays, for instance, in London and at Oxford, what was being tested was obviously the capacity of the modern stage to represent, in any adequate measure or degree, works of introspective method and strange or sterile psychology. But the artistic value of* Strafford, *or* In a Balcony, *was settled when Robert Browning wrote their last lines. It is not, Sir, by the mimes that the muses are to be judged.*

So far, the writer of the article in question is right. Where he goes wrong is in saying that I described this frame—the stage—as being furnished "with a set of puppets". He admits that he speaks only by report; but he should have remembered, Sir, that report is not merely a lying jade, which I personally would readily forgive her, but a jade who lies without lovely invention—a thing that I, at any rate, can forgive her never.

What I really said was that the frame we call the stage was "peopled with either living actors or moving puppets", and I pointed out briefly, of necessity, that the personality of the actor is often a source of danger in the perfect presentation of a work of art. It may distort. It may lead astray. It may be a discord in the tone or symphony. For anybody can act. Most people in England do nothing else. To be conventional is to be a comedian. To act a particular part, however, is a very different thing, and a very difficult thing as well. The actor's aim is, or should be, to convert his own accidental personality into the real and essential personality of the character he is called upon to impersonate, whatever that character may be; or perhaps I should say that there are two schools of actors— the school of those who attain their effect by exaggeration of personality, and the school of those who attain it by suppression. It would be too long to discuss these schools, or to decide which of them the dramatist loves best. Let me note the danger of personality, and pass on to my puppets.

There are many advantages in puppets. They never argue. They have no crude views about art. They have no private lives. We are never bothered by accounts of their virtues, or bored by recitals of their vices; and when they are out of an engagement they never do good in public, or save people from drowning; nor do they speak more than is set down for them. They recognise the presiding intellect of the dramatist, and have never been known to ask for their parts to be written up. They are admirably docile, and have no personalities at all. I saw lately, in Paris, a performance by certain puppets of Shakespeare's Tempest, *in M. Maurice Boucher's translation. Miranda was the image of Miranda, because an artist had so fashioned her; and Ariel was true Ariel, because so had she been made. Their gestures were quite sufficient, and the words that seemed to come from their little lips were spoken by poets who had beautiful voices. It was a delightful performance, and I remember it still with delight, though Miranda took no notice of the flowers I sent her after the curtain fell. For modern plays, however, perhaps we had better have living players, for in modern plays actuality is everything. The charm—the ineffable charm—of the unreal is here denied us, and rightly.*

I remain, Sir, your obedient servant,

OSCAR WILDE

LONDON, 19*th February*

And here the Little Books end, with Irving still plain Mister.

The Envelopes

IN 1895 criticism had become once more a serious art. The palmy days of Hazlitt (1778 - 1830) and G. H. Lewes (1817 - 1878) had been succeeded by, to mix the metaphor, the doldrums of both playwriting and play-criticising. The nineteenth century had been a period largely made up of decay and disappointment. Its early years saw the retirement of Mrs. Siddons and John Philip Kemble, with whom the grand style of acting definitely passed away. Great actors of other styles abounded, but there was an almost complete lack of good playwrights to support even good second-rate players. Sheridan Knowles and Bulwer Lytton succeeded plentifully in falling between two stools— the bombastic throne to which their genius was unequal and the domestic chair which they had not common sense enough to fill. But then the domestic chair was as yet hardly in evidence. Knowles died in 1862, and Lytton eleven years later. It was in 1838 and the two following years that Bulwer wrote the three works which were his masterpieces—*The Lady of Lyons, Richelieu* and *Money*. It is always quaintly said of these plays that they have kept the stage ever since. What this means I do not know. There is no living actor or actress who could cope with the rodomontade of Pauline and her lover, and if there were, modern taste would not put up with them. I know of no performances in recent years with the exception of "command" performances, or performances for charity. Professor Morley has an admirable description of the state of the English stage during the years which preceded the coming of Robertson, and I imagine that a great deal that he wrote then would hold good even in our own time. "There is," says Morley, "a large half-intelligent population that by bold puffing can be got into a theatre. It numbers golden lads and lassies as well as chimney-sweeps. The population is, indeed, so large that it takes many nights to pass it through a theatre, each night's theatre-full being as a bucket-full dipped out of a big stagnant pond. Any manager may, if he will, set his face against intelligent opinion, and, falling back upon the half-intelligent, go the right way to that pond, bale patiently and send nearly the whole of it through his house. . . . Against the condemnation of his piece by every educated man he can set the advertisement that Duchesses and Viscounts have been to see it, and that it is being acted for its millionth night." All of which applies very accurately to present-day conditions. The whole of theatrical history in the 'fifties and 'sixties is the history of the inferior works of the French stage; nearly all English plays of the period are translations or adaptations from what the Professor so felicitously calls *Pomme Pourrie* by MM. Péché and Bonbon.

Enfin Robertson vint. Born in 1829, he was thirty-five years old when he committed the crime known as *David Garrick*, for which he was sentenced to be acted by amateurs for ever. The following year saw *Society* produced at, and Society flocking to, the Prince of Wales Theatre. This little house in Tottenham Street was under the management of Marie Wilton, afterwards Mrs., and later Lady, Bancroft. *Ours* was produced in 1866, *Caste* in 1867, *Play* in 1868, *School* in 1869, *M.P.* in 1870. Of these *Caste* still "holds the stage," in the sense that performances are given from time to time for money and not out of mere curiosity. Those who are interested may like to note that in the year in which *Caste* was produced, Browning published *The Ring and the Book*, Dickens was at work upon his last novel, and William Morris was writing the first volumes of *The Earthly Paradise*.

For some time yet it seemed as though these plays of Robertson's were to be the only realistic stones cast into the pool of balderdash. The success of H. J. Byron's *Our Boys*, which ran at the Vaudeville Theatre from January, 1875, till April, 1879, plunged the stage into a flood of Byronism of the worst sort. As an actor Byron had neither originality nor charm; as a playwright he was hardly more than a punster.

Then within three years appeared three plays by three writers, two of whom were to have an immense influence on the English commercial theatre as distinct from the theatre of ideas. Only, of course, one must always credit our commercial theatre with sufficient gumption to take up with her less fashionable sister for such period as there is any money in her. That is why the "problem plays" of Arthur Wing Pinero and Henry Arthur Jones were so successful. English society, having heard vaguely of Ibsen's problematic heroes and heroines, was all agog to have expounded to it problems of its own people. Pinero and Jones obliged accordingly with theses suited to Mayfair's mood, tacking on to them solutions whose essential falsity made them extremely palatable to the modish playgoer. Vanity was tickled at being asked to think in the theatre without any loss of complacency resulting from that thought. In the meantime we must go back to our three little plays—Pinero's *Two Hundred a Year*, which appeared in 1877, Jones's *Only Round the Corner*, produced in 1878, and Sydney Grundy's *The Snowball*, staged in 1879.

Grundy is easily disposed of. He wrote nothing that will live because he never wrote anything that was alive. *A Pair of Spectacles* (1890) was sentimental melodrama freely adapted from *Les Petits Oiseaux* of Labiche and Delacour; *A Fool's Paradise* (1892) was a pure domestic tragedy; *Sowing the Wind* (1893) had to do with illegitimate children; and *A Bunch of Violets* (1894), for which the author went to Octave Feuillet, was a "melodramatic domestic problem drama." In the last two plays Grundy was certainly tarred, as Clement Scott would have said, with the Ibsen brush. But this playwright had no mind, and one feels that he chose to deal in pitch only because defilement was *à la mode*.

Perhaps the English theatre can give no more significant proof of growth than the general use in the 'nineties of the phrase, "the problem play." To-day we take it for granted that a piece shall state some problem in life, conduct or manners. The problem is not necessarily sexual, and we do not spend our evenings debating whether the children of syphilitic parents should take one another in marriage. Wassermann has settled that question. To-day we ask whether there is a spirit-land, and whether in the next world a mother who died when her son was a baby will be glad to welcome a strapping middle-aged man with quarter-deck manners (*Mary Rose*). Or whether mothers should encourage their sons to dope (*The Vortex*). Or whether the French had not plentiful reason to thank the English for ridding them of their turbulent priestess (*Saint Joan*). Before the 'nineties it had never entered the heads of playgoers that they might be called upon to use those heads, and when they were so called upon they grew portentous and talked of "problems"; to-day we presume that the play is for beings with power of ratiocination unless the words "light" or "farcical" comedy warn us to the contrary.

The problem play, so called, was first ushered into the commercial theatre in England by Pinero's *The Second Mrs. Tanqueray* (1893) and continued in vogue with Jones's *Michael and his Lost Angel* (1896). But there was an enormous amount of playwriting in this country between the last flicker of Byron's punning and the first flicker of the intellectual drama. There was Oscar Wilde, first-rate wit and man of the theatre, second-rate poet and tenth-rate everything else. As a dramatist Wilde was like an architect who should be so highly absorbed in his ornamentations that he forgot his constructions; there is no play of his which would not have fallen down if he had not relied upon some older builder to put its bricks together for him. His plots are hoary with the dexterity of previous generations.

Then there was Haddon Chambers, a popular playwright, who achieved a number of comedies of sentiment and satire of which the best-known is *The Idler* (1891) and the best-written *The Tyranny of Tears* (1899). This playwright accomplished the bulk of his work before 1900, only four plays coming from his pen between that date and 1921, when he died.

Prior to 1893 Pinero had written fifteen plays which to-day are only names and hardly that. In 1885 he inaugurated with *The Magistrate* that series of brilliant farces which are equal to the best of Labiche, bringing the series to an end in 1893 with *The Amazons*. These little pieces show this playwright as a first-class man of the theatre and a *vaudevilliste* of genius. In 1893 Pinero produced *The Second Mrs. Tanqueray*, which proved none of the things it set out to prove, and demonstrated a lot that the author never intended— that marriage with an *exalté* like Aubrey Tanqueray is an infliction beyond the endurance of any woman of spirit, respectable or otherwise, that life in an English country house must inevitably lead to suicide, and that "under a queer fantastic light at night or in the glare of the morning, that horrid, irresistible truth that physical repulsion forces on men and women" will come to Tanqueray, and he will realise that Paula has "gone off" in the same way as, and no differently from, Mrs. Cortelyon or any other decent woman. As a warning to adventuresses the play was a failure—that Cyprian would indeed be lacking in dash who boggled at the million-to-one chance of a former protector falling in love with his successor's daughter. As a tragedy it failed also—there being nothing particularly tragic or even impolite about Ardale's union with Ellean. But Pinero is such a master of the stage in all things not of the first importance that the play, in conjunction with the great talent of Mrs. Patrick Campbell, had an immense success. The hypercritical may say that Pinero, having taken the trouble to learn Ibsen's language, was in this piece heard to speak it indifferently, but the fact remains that *The Second Mrs. Tanqueray* is a great stage-play which, in spite and perhaps because of its evasions, has always had the power to move an audience so long as there has been an actress with the power to play Paula. But suppose that flamboyant lady had chosen to go off again with Ardale and leave Aubrey and Ellean to an interchange of priggish consolation? Or that

Photo: "The Theatre"

Edward Terry

Photo: copied by Howard M. King

Mrs. Patrick Campbell in "The Notorious Mrs. Ebbsmith"

Paula had discovered Tanqueray to be the father not of a grown-up daughter, but of a grown-up son to whom she "was not a stranger"? Or simply that she had decided that she could not "stick" respectability whether Ardale turned up or not, and had taken the next train back to Claridge's or whatever hotel was in vogue in 1893? Would the audience have embraced a living woman as they embraced one who committed suicide for no discoverable reason? The answer is in the negative. A real live Paula would have been immoral. One who commits suicide needed no whitewashing.

In *Michael and his Lost Angel*, Henry Arthur Jones put another question and, like his confrère, ran away from the answer. Of this piece G.B.S. remarked: "As to the first two acts, I ask nothing better; but at the beginning of the third comes the parting of our ways; and I can point out the exact place where the roads fork. In the first act, Michael, a clergyman, compels a girl who has committed what he believes to be a deadly sin, to confess it publicly in church. In the second act he commits that sin himself. At the beginning of the third act he meets the lady who has been his accomplice; and the following words pass between them:

"AUDRIE.   You're sorry?

"MICHAEL.   No. And you?

"AUDRIE.   No.

"Now, after this, what does the clergyman do? Without giving another thought to the all-significant fact that he is not sorry—that at the very point where, if his code and creed were valid, his conscience would be aching with remorse, he is not only impenitent, but positively glad, he proceeds to act as if he really were penitent, and not only puts on a hair shirt, but actually makes a confession to his congregation in the false character of a contrite sinner, and goes out from among them with bowed head to exile and disgrace, only waiting in the neighbourhood until the church is empty to steal back and privily contradict his pious imposture by picking up and hiding a flower which the woman has thrown on the steps of the altar."

In other words the solution to the situation was pure tosh. But there is this to be said for the playwright—that he did at least have the courage to state his situation, the date being 1896. In the theatre the play obtained a very fair amount of success. For the plays of Pinero and Jones, whatever else they may not be, are always exciting after the manner of those newspapers which never fail to make the reader believe that something of importance happened yesterday. The years between 1893 and 1900 are noteworthy principally for the increasing prowess of these two playwrights. During this time Pinero wrote *The Notorious Mrs. Ebbsmith*, *The Benefit of the Doubt*, *The Princess and the Butterfly*, *Trelawny of the Wells*, and *The Gay Lord Quex*, while Jones's principal contribution was that brilliant comedy *The Liars*. Both these playwrights, it cannot be too strongly insisted, were masters of the theatre. Both showed an immense advance in technique and subject-matter upon the theatre of Robertson, Boucicault, Taylor and Grundy. In their hands the intellectual gap between the English novel and the English drama was lessened from a hundred years to fifty.

And with the new movement came the new critics. Henry Morley and Dutton Cook had gone, and Clement Scott was going. They were succeeded by G.B.S., William Archer, Max and J. T. Grein—the most brilliant critical galaxy that has ever coruscated at one and the same time. The Envelopes begin with a mighty dollop of Archer on *The Notorious Mrs. Ebbsmith*. Indeed, with two dollops, since that redoubtable Scot needed two weeks in which to empty his mind on Pinero's teaser.

20th and 27th March, 1895

The new play is in all essentials a great advance on *The Second Mrs. Tanqueray*. Those critics who take the opposite view are in reality hankering after the more commonplace and melodramatic elements in the earlier play. In it we had character precipitated by external coincidence; here we have character working itself out entirely from within. Moreover, Mr. Pinero has here chosen a much more vital theme. Most of us can afford to take a very abstract interest in the theory of marriage with a demi-rep. We know in advance that it is a hazardous experiment—that the county people won't call, while the lady's former associates probably will. Thus *The Second Mrs. Tanqueray* is really little more than the portrait of Paula—a brilliant piece of work, but isolated, almost irrelevant. In *The Notorious Mrs. Ebbsmith*, on the other hand, Mr. Pinero goes straight for the universally relevant theme of marriage in general, and draws three characters in place of one. It is unfair to complain that his treatment of the theme is inconclusive. If it had been "conclusive," on one side or other, those who dissented would have dubbed Mr. Pinero a "faddist" and complained of being preached at. What he has conclusively shown is that, as society is at present constituted, it takes exceptional characters on both sides to make a free union any more successful than a marriage. This is not a very difficult point to prove;

but as a contribution to the philosophy of the subject, it is at least as valid as Mr. Grant Allen's contention that two people of perfect character may form an ideal union "without benefit of clergy", especially if one of the parties will have the good taste to die of typhoid before time has tested the strength of the bond.

The design of the play, then, is above reproach. It is technically by far the strongest thing our modern stage has to show. An expository character or two might perhaps be dispensed with, and an over-nicety of explanation as to the comings and goings of the personages might possibly have been avoided; but these are the veriest trivialities. The main fact is that we have a drama consisting simply in the interaction of two characters, developing itself through four acts, without situations, revelations, starts, surprises, or picture-poster attractions of any sort, yet from first to last enthralling the attention and stimulating the intelligence. Stimulating, I say, not always satisfying; for when we come to look into the characters we cannot but doubt whether Mr. Pinero has quite achieved what he seems to have intended. Lucas Cleeve is admirable—the man of facile enthusiasms and discouragements, "possessing ambition without patience, self-esteem without confidence"—but Agnes Ebbsmith, however vividly and ably projected, can scarcely pass muster as a well-observed type. Mr. Pinero has not entered with sympathetic clairvoyance into the mental history and habit—he has not even mastered the vocabulary, the jargon, if you will—of the class of woman he sets out to portray. I suspect him of holding "views" as to feminine human nature in general; and "views," like knotty window-panes, are fatal to observation. In this he is by no means alone. Nine-tenths of masculine woman-drawing is vitiated by "views"—and, in these latter days, about nineteen-twentieths of feminine woman-drawing. You may think it a reckless paradox, but Ibsen seems to me one of the few modern writers whose studies of feminine character are undistorted by "views." He does not go to work syllogistically, saying to himself, "All women are this, that, and the other thing; my heroine is a woman; therefore she is this, that, and the other thing." He looks straight at and through women, and draws them in their infinite variety. Time was when he, too, held views, and then he drew *his* Agnes, and other characters of that order. They were beautiful in their time, but he has gone far beyond them. Ten years hence we may perhaps be saying the same of Mr. Pinero's Agnes.

She is the daughter, so she says, of a revolutionary Socialist, atheist, and all the rest of it; yet her whole habit of mind is that of one who has been steeped from the outset in orthodoxy, and has embraced heterodoxy in fear and trembling, with a sense of strangeness and adventure. "In spite of father's unbelief and mother's indifference," she says, "I was in my heart as devout as any girl in a parsonage. . . . Whenever I could escape from our stifling rooms at home, the air blew away uncertainty and scepticism." We are told of no external influence that made her regard her father's ideas as "strange", and think of his paganism as "scepticism". Mr. Pinero seems to assume "devoutness" as a sort of universal instinct of the childish, or at any rate of the woman-childish, heart, and to conceive that this instinct alone would prevent the ideas of a much-loved father from "soaking into" his daughter. Now, as a matter of fact (I don't think Mr. Diggle himself would deny this), your ordinary child is instinctively an out-and-out pagan. The childish criticism of the universe is remorselessly rationalistic. It is religion, not irreligion, that a child requires to be taught. The father's agnosticism might not soak very deep into the child, and might be effectually counteracted by some other and more positive influence; but we hear of nothing of the sort. It is even possible that, by some freak of atavism, like that which makes the daughter of Mr. Grant Allen's *Woman who Did* an incurable little snob and numskull, the atheist father and indifferent mother might produce a daughter with a constitutional bent towards mysticism, an innate genius for piety. But that is not Agnes's case. For fourteen years of her mature life she has been a pagan; for six of them she has been an active propagandist; she conceives herself to be still a pagan at the very moment when, by talking of "uncertainty and scepticism", "hope and faith", she shows that she regards religious belief as the normal and fundamental attitude of the human mind. Now, whether this be so or not, it is certainly the last thing that a woman like Agnes would admit or assume. Her spiritual history does not hang together. It is not probably constructed or possibly expressed. Mr. Pinero has failed to put himself in the position of what may be called a congenital pagan—a woman who from childhood has taken in rationalism at the pores of her skin, as most children take in Christianity. Yet that, for aught we can see or reasonably conjecture, is precisely Agnes's case. It seems to be Mr. Pinero's belief that "every woman is at heart a"—saint. The Bible incident, I take it, at the end of the third act, symbolises his "view" that no woman is strong enough to go through life without some supernatural refuge to fly to in time of need; so that, even if she thinks she has cast her "hope and faith" into the fire, she will presently pluck them out again, though she sear her flesh in the attempt. Well, there are instances that favour that view, and I think there are instances against it. But though we may cite women who preach atheism to-day, and go to confession or to Thibet to-morrow, while they *are* secularists they stand at, and speak from, the secularist's point of view. Agnes Ebbsmith, on the other hand, even in expounding her heterodoxy, unconsciously adopts the standpoint and uses the language of orthodoxy.

Equally unrealised are her sociological doctrines. John Thorold, for instance, must have been a very strange Socialist if his daughter ever heard him talking about "division of wealth, and the rest of it." That is the language of the gentleman who writes to *The Times* to point out that, if all property were equally divided to-day, there would be rich men and poor men to-morrow, millionaires and paupers the day after. This Socialist daughter of a Socialist does not know the phraseology of her party. Again, her objections to marriage are curiously—shall I say empirical? Because her father and mother and "most of our married friends" lived a cat-and-dog life, and because her own husband was a brute, she sets forth to preach Free Union as the panacea for a cantankerous world. It does not seem to enter her head that there are drawbacks to marriage even between people of reasonably good tempers, good hearts, and good manners. Of the economic, ethical, and sentimental common-places of attack upon marriage, which a woman in her position would be bound to have at her fingers' ends, she appears to know nothing. It is especially noteworthy that she ignores the question of children, as affecting the relation of the sexes. The world of her speculations is a childless world. A triangle, in her trigonometry, consists of two straight lines. Her struggle, too, against what she calls "passion", seems to me to show a misconception on Mr. Pinero's part of the type of woman with whom he is dealing—or rather a confusion of two distinct types. He thinks vaguely of rebellion against the primary conditions of sex as a general characteristic of the "new" or advanced woman. Now there are—or rather there have been, for the type is surely "going out"— women constitutionally inaccessible to passion, who resent it as a degrading servitude, and would fain make their individual limitation a law, or an ideal, for their fellow-women. But such women would be the last to enter on a free union. Married they may be—they may have taken on the yoke before they realised their own temperament, or they may have condescended to marriage for the sake of its social and economic advantages. But love, in the largest sense of the word, is as incomprehensible to them as passion. They do not want even the friendship or close companionship of a man. Their instinct is to make their own sex as nearly as possible self-sufficing. Why, then, should they incur all sorts of social disadvantages for the sake of a companionship which they do not require or desire? And, in any case, Agnes is clearly not a creature of this brood. She is not naturally a passionless woman. She loves Lucas, in the fullest sense of the word, with a love that survives even her fuller insight into his character. Her inspiration towards a "colder, more temperate, more impassive companionship" is a merely intellectual vagary, and I venture to think that it springs from a misconception on Mr. Pinero's part. Newspaper moralists have so persistently prefixed the stereotypes "sexless" and "unsexed" to the "new woman" that he has been betrayed into grafting an inconsistent attribute upon his heroine's character. The real, or, at any rate, the characteristic, "new woman" accepts with something more than equanimity the destinies of her sex, and would certainly not ignore the possibility of motherhood in her rearrangement of the scheme of things. One could understand Agnes's position if her previous experience of marriage had given her such a horror of "passion" that she had resolved from the very outset to maintain her companionship with Lucas on a supersexual basis. But we are told in so many words that this is not the case. Her rebellion against passion is an afterthought, and surely an improbable one. It might pass as a whim of the moment, but such a whim should be the subject of a comedietta, not of a serious play.

Perhaps you think that, if these criticisms are justified, there is very little of Agnes left. But when you see the play you will discover that they are more verbal than essential—that in order to obviate them only a few changes of phraseology would be required, the main lines of the action, the fundamental processes of emotion, remaining unaltered. I, for my part, flatly dissent from that "view" of Mr. Pinero's, to which we owe the Bible incident and the pietistic end; but, after all, he has a perfect right to hold and illustrate this view. For the rest, *The Notorious Mrs. Ebbsmith* seems to me the work of a born and highly accomplished dramatist, who goes right essentially and by instinct, and wrong superficially, for lack of special knowledge. It should be quite possible to tell Agnes's story, up to the moment when she thrusts her hand into the fire, without altering a single incident or emotion, yet in such a way as to obviate all the above objections, which are founded upon phrases rather than facts. But here I must break off a discussion which has already exceeded all bounds. I hope to resume it in another article, and to say something of the acting.

✻   ✻   ✻   ✻   ✻   ✻

After pointing out, last week, what seem to me certain errors of observation in the character of Agnes Ebbsmith, I stated my belief that these errors are verbal rather than essential. It should be possible, I said, to tell Agnes's story, at any rate up to the end of the third act, without altering any incident or emotion, yet in such a way as to obviate all my criticisms. Let me now make the attempt; repeating, however, that my—what shall I call it?—my exposition stops short at the Bible incident. To account for that, it would be necessary to introduce a new element into Agnes's previous history; and that is against the rules of the game.

Well, then—she is the daughter of a Socialist orator, has imbibed her father's religious and political ideas, and has seen, in her home life, the miseries of an ill-assorted marriage. Nevertheless, she marries early, to find herself her husband's sultana for one year and his servant for seven—at the end of which period he dies. Confirmed, by her personal ill-hap, in her allegiance to her father's ideas, she becomes an active propagandist of social democracy and female emancipation; but losing her voice and being in the pinch of poverty, she takes to nursing as a means of livelihood, and in the course of her duties comes across Lucas Cleeve. All this is probable enough, and all this is precisely what Agnes relates of herself. It is not in the facts, but in her wording of them that the improbability comes in. She speaks of both free-thought and Socialism, not as one to the manner born, but rather as one not yet acclimatised, and ignorant of technicalities and shibboleths. Lucas Cleeve (to return to the story) is in the hot fit of rebellion against marriage with a hard-natured worldly woman who despises him instead of bringing him the sympathy and appreciation for which his weak egoism craves. These qualities, together with a tender unworldliness, he finds in Agnes. Illness and distance make his old life and its ambitions and interests seem infinitely aloof from him, and he is quite ready to be infected by the enthusiasms of this stately creature, the antithesis in every respect of the wife who has wounded him. He loves in her a "ministering angel", and she a convert in him. So they cast in their lots together, and we find them in Venice. But now, as Lucas regains strength, and as the decisive moment approaches when he must break once for all with his traditions and his career, the habits of his caste reassert themselves, and he finds his enthusiasm for free union in the abstract, and for social democracy in the concrete, rapidly cooling. He still loves Agnes, but not as she longs to be loved. He loves her in spite of, not in and for, her ideas. She gradually comes to feel that her aspirations towards "plain living and high thinking," towards labour, and if need be martyrdom, for social emancipation and justice, are in

his eyes little better than eccentricities of which she must be gradually
cured. He would have her put on the gowns and the prejudices of his
caste. She sees, with deep humiliation, that she holds him by his senses,
not by his intellect; that they are not fellow-workers in a great cause,
not shining examples of a high ideal, but are simply living in vulgar vice,
a rich young profligate and his mistress. On realising this, she tries to save
her self-respect by raising their companionship to a purely intellectual
and supersexual plane; so that even this recrudescence of the innate
puritanism of the English middle classes becomes comprehensible enough
if we take it, not as a general characteristic of the type of woman
Mr. Pinero is portraying, but as resulting from the special circumstances
of Agnes's case. At this juncture the Duke of St. Olpherts comes on the
scene, a living embodiment of all those forces in Lucas's nature against
which Agnes is carrying on a despairing battle. She knows that what
seemed eccentric in Lucas's own eyes will appear grotesque and hateful
when seen in the concave mirror of the Duke's scepticism. She seeks an
encounter with the Duke so as to know and measure her adversary.
To say that such a woman would not "Trafalgar Square" him in her
own drawing-room is absurd. There is a great deal of human nature
even in collectivists, and it would be a foolish affectation on her part
to treat the Duke as though they met on the neutral territory of ordinary
social intercourse. The verbal form of her "Trafalgar Squaring" may be
open to criticism; the fact is natural and even inevitable. Having gauged
the Duke's strength, she sees that she must either give up the battle or
fight him with his own weapons. To give it up would be not only to
lose a convert and shatter a still fascinating dream but to submit to the
soiling of her life with a futile and degrading episode. It is tolerable, it
may even be piquant, not to be a man's first love; it is intolerably
humiliating not to be his last. So she determines to fight the Duke—the
World, the Flesh, and the Devil incarnate—with his own weapons. She
has wit and beauty; she will use them! She puts off the "dowdy
demagogue" and puts on the bewitching woman; and hey presto! Faust
is at her feet again and Mephistopheles is apparently routed. And now,
to her own surprise, she finds herself, for a moment, thrilling with the
joy of triumph—and of surrender. "Her sex has found her out"; she
knows that it is no longer the convert she loves in Lucas, but the man;
and beneath her sense of treachery to her ideals, she is conscious of a
tremulous delight. It was in this phase of the character that Mrs. Patrick
Campbell's otherwise brilliant performance seemed to me to fall a little
short. It may be that I am refining too much upon Mr. Pinero's

conception, but I can certainly see nothing *in*consistent with a reading more subtle and at the same time more human than Mrs. Campbell's. The actress seemed to feel only the irony in Agnes's thoughts, not the genuine underlying joy. There was nothing but bitterness in her realisation that her "woman's one hour" had come; and that I cannot take to have been the author's meaning. It is true that Agnes had expected her hour to come in a very different shape; but her sentiment on finding that it has taken her by surprise is surely not one of mere disgust and discontent. Mrs. Campbell seemed to me to ignore in effect, as she certainly delivered without conviction, that outburst of Agnes's in answer to the Duke's wish that Lucas were "a different sort of feller"—"Nothing matters now—not even that. He's mine. He would have died but for me. I gave him life. He is my child, my husband, my lover, my bread, my daylight—all—everything. Mine. Mine." Beautiful and fascinating as Mrs. Campbell undoubtedly was throughout, I could not but find a certain superficiality, hardness, almost shrewishness, in her treatment of the third act. Agnes's "hour", at any rate, is a very brief one. Lucas has not sense enough to realise her sacrifice. Finding her, as he thinks, "gowned" and in her right mind, he must needs take the opportunity to insult and exult over the ideals and aspirations which were to have been the bond of union between them; and she sees that at best she has to face a second cycle of passion and satiety, like that of her first marriage. Then, putting him to the test with death in her heart, she finds him prepared for, and even hankering after, a squalid compromise, in which she, instead of making her life a proud and open protest against the slavery of marriage, is to join the furtive horde of mercenary irregulars who smooth the way for the triumphant march of the hymeneal legion. At this her soul revolts; and leaving behind her the four words, "My hour is over," she departs from the palace of her daydream, which has become in her eyes a house of shame.

Have I kept my promise? Frankly, I think so. I have told the story of a very true, very subtle, and very tragic play, a play which none but a master dramatist could have invented and composed; and it is simply Mr. Pinero's play up to the last five minutes of the third act, with nothing added, and nothing essential left out. It is the play you can see every night at the Garrick Theatre, somewhat, but very slightly, obscured by a few unrealised phrases placed in Agnes's mouth. Mr. Pinero, I take it, is much in the position of (say) a clergyman of great ability, insight, and literary power, who should undertake to write a novel of stage-life, having an actress for its heroine, with no more intimate knowledge of the stage, and its ways of thought and speech, than may be gained from a few casual visits to the Lyceum stalls. He might quite well draw a very true and fascinating woman, though an unconvincing actress; and Agnes, in the same way, is a very true and fascinating woman, though an unconvincing Socialist and Secularist. I wish the play ended, as it might very well, at the point where my narrative leaves off. It is at this point that Mr. Pinero's preconceived "view" of feminine character intervenes, to my thinking, rather disastrously. I see no reason why Agnes should throw the Bible into the fire, no reason why she should pluck it out again. That seems to me the culmination of another play, another character-study. As for the great scene of the last act—the scene between Agnes and Sybil Cleeve—it is a daring and scathing piece of satire, but somewhat of a superfluity none the less. Agnes's acquiescence in Sybil's proposal simply takes my breath away. I can trace it only to a queer survival of the heroic-self-sacrifice superstition which inspired so many of the French sentimental dramas of twenty years ago. One might almost say of it, as Dr. Johnson said of the *Beggar's Opera:* "There is in it such a labefaction of all principles as may be injurious to morality."

With the opening of Her Majesty's Theatre a few months earlier Herbert Beerbohm Tree had come into the picture.

28th April, 1897

A sense that they were assisting at something more than an ordinary first-night's function seemed to animate those present at the opening of the new theatre erected for Mr. Tree, on the site formerly occupied by the King's Theatre, or as it was subsequently known, Her Majesty's Theatre, in the Haymarket. Everything conceivable was indeed done to furnish a ceremonial worthy of so important an occasion, and the proceedings generally were impressive, and are likely to remain memorable. The first step or act consisted of the delivery by Mrs. Tree of the sparkling and happy occasional address of the Laureate. The poem, happily rhymed and vigorously written, and full of patriotic allusions, stirred deeply the audience.

> "Leaving life's load of dulness at the door,
>   You come to dwell in fairyland once more.
>   Puck, Ariel, Pegasus, imp, fairy, sprite,
>   All that can lend illusion and delight,

Quick to come forth and frolic as you bid,
Behind that curtain cunningly are hid.
We have the Muses nine, the Graces three,
And all the passions—under lock and key.
Which would you summon? Laughter, terror, tears?
Call each in turn, and promptly it appears.

For this we put on motley to the view,
And travesty ourselves to comfort you.
Yet there is one, whose venerated name
We humbly borrow, and will never shame,
Who needs no tinsel trappings nor disguise
To shine a monarch in the whole world's eyes,
Waits for no prompter for the timely word,
And, when 'tis uttered, everywhere is heard;
Plays, through sheer goodness, a commanding part,
Speaks from the soul, and acts but from the heart.
Long may she linger, loved, upon the scene,
And long resound the prayer, 'God save our
                gracious Queen!' "

The curtain opening then revealed a stage filled with the artists and chorus of the house, by whom "God Save the Queen" was sung, the solos being taken by Miss Butt. An extra verse, assigned to Longfellow, and embodying a prayer for peace, the appropriateness of which was realised by the audience, was introduced. The whole of the numbers of the ceremonial was received with the utmost enthusiasm, the audience cheering for several minutes. This constituted, with the addition of the speech wrung from Mr. Tree at the close, the whole of the ceremonial.

After the opening portion of the ceremony had been got through, the curtain drew up on the prologue to Mr. Gilbert Parker's *Seats of the Mighty*. Though a novelty on this side of the water, the play has been seen in America, where its merits and defects have been keenly debated. Its reception in England was friendly and enthusiastic, even though the feeling of those present was that it probably formed a convenient rather than a judicious choice for an opening experiment. It has theatrical situations and scenes, and furnishes opportunity for some novel and stirring historical pageants, as well as for picturesque court and military costumes. Its construction is, however, cumbrous, and its development of story, not too easy to follow to those familiar with the book, is positively difficult to those with no such knowledge. But for the original and well-conceived character, which Mr. Parker has strangely named Doltaire, the play would scarcely have commended itself to the management. Doltaire seems intended to combine in his own nature the various forces which led to the French Revolution. The son of Louis XV by the daughter of a Poictiers gardener or farm labourer, he represents the worst aspects of one of the most heartless, dissipated, and corrupt of Courts, and yet has a plebeian revolt against the iniquitous laws, which give all to the courtier and the noble, and deprive the peasant almost of the right to live. An associate of philosophers, he has adopted their profane and cynical creed, and believes in nothing as worthy or of high repute. This character, a compound of Mephistopheles and Voltaire, has commended itself to Mr. Tree, who has introduced into it some humanising traits. With a view, it may be supposed, to assigning Doltaire a certain measure of sympathy, Mr. Tree shows him in a prologue, which is not in the original, and is located, so far as its action is concerned, in Versailles, as moved by the sufferings of the poor, from whom on one side at least he springs. In order to assign him histrionic importance, the actor has made him deliver in 1759 a prophecy concerning the approaching revolution, in which its full horrors are foretold. It is from the acting rather than the psychological standpoint, moreover, that he has humanised his love for Alixe, the heroine, and has shown a commonplace and even conventional jealousy as underlying his persecution of the hero, Captain Moray. The appreciation of the undaunted courage of his opponent, which is a striking feature in the Doltaire of the original book, disappears. It is a striking, picturesque, and impressive figure that remains, and is warmly commended to us by the impersonation of Mr. Tree, who shows with equal power and intensity its picturesque, its chivalric, and its malignant aspects. The mocking and cynical side is that on which Mr. Tree most insists. It is difficult to imagine words spoken with a subtler and more effective mixture of causticity, insolence, courtesy, and contempt than he employs.

With the story of the play it is needless long to concern ourselves. Captain Moray possesses compromising documents of Mdme. de Pompadour, and is a prisoner in Quebec. A reluctant agent of the King's mistress, Doltaire comes to Quebec for the purpose of obtaining these missives. In the discharge of this trust, he finds that the Englishman who refuses to surrender the coveted documents is a favoured rival. Again and again he condemns to death the man whose obstinacy irritates him as much as his rivalry inflames him. As often the Englishman's life is saved by the fair and devoted Alixe. In the end the English, directed by Captain Moray, who in some not very conceivable fashion has escaped, storm the Heights of Abraham, and Quebec is captured. The death of Doltaire is due to an accident, he being the victim of a revenge directed against another man. The chapel in which he has taken refuge is undermined and blown up, while through the crevices in the ruined walls we see the tall, quaint headgear of the British troops surmounting the hill crest, hearing at the same time the strains of the pibroch and of *The Men of Harlech*, and the blare of the English trumpets. By what incidents or suggestions the story is illuminated we will not pause to tell. We are shown the Court at Versailles, with the revels in honour of the Pompadour, and hear the fierce mob without the gates of the citadel at Quebec clamouring for bread at the moment when their companions with misdirected energy are firing the granaries. We find Frenchmen and women, from the Mistress of the Court downwards, intriguing to sell State secrets and pocket English gold. In these separate pictures, rather than in the uninterrupted flow of action or the heat begotten of sympathy with devotion and suffering, the chief attraction is found. Meantime, the spectacle is beautiful, stimulating, and the dresses are a dream. Leaving to Miss Janette Steer the part of the insidious and treacherous Mdme. de Pompadour, Mrs. Tree takes the character of a dancer, inflamed by jealousy, in which her higher gifts are seen to advantage, and from which she expresses the utmost possible. Miss Kate Rorke presents, with exquisite and unsurpassable sweetness, the rôle of Alixe, which, however, furnishes few opportunities, except in a scene recalling Richard III and Lady Anne. Mr. Charles Brookfield gives a striking picture of Louis XV; Mr. Lewis Waller is duly chivalrous and uncompromising as Captain Moray, who coquets with death in a manner more quixotic than sensible or well-advised. Mr. Murray Carson, Mr. Charles Allan, and many other admirably competent actors took part in a performance which leaves nothing to be desired. The whole was received with marked favour, and Mr. Tree was the recipient of a tremendous greeting. At the close he came forward and spoke a few words of thanks.

FORBES-ROBERTSON IN *HAMLET*

And now Forbes-Robertson makes history.

11th September, 1897

Forbes Robertson brings to his task all the admirable and invaluable equipments of the actor. His noble voice, capable of every tone and modulation, is priceless. It can be alternately deep and tender. It reminds one of the moan and wail of the "cello." He does not attempt to make himself fanciful or pretty. He wears his own hair, which so well suits his clear-cut and intellectual countenance, and he does not bedizen himself all over with stars and decorations and coloured orders. In fact, it would not be wrong to say that the Hamlet looked a little "dowdy" in his suit of rusty black, unadorned and unrelieved. But it only emphasised the more the striking force of the face, on which every passion, every doubt, and each anxiety were deeply registered. What then—apart from new readings, or old readings, or omissions from the text, or what not—were the salient features of the newest of all the new Hamlets? We should say two things. First, his consummate good breeding, united with frankness of nature and lovableness of disposition. Secondly, a mind deeply sensitive to religious impression. We can conceive such a Hamlet to have been idolised by his fellow-students—to have been their "chum" and their model of a downright "good fellow." It is with difficulty that he throws away this boyish impetuosity when confronted with the horror of the situation in which he is involved. Over and over again it bubbles up and bursts the bounds of will-power to subdue it—this keen sense of humour, this desperate, natural, impulsive *joie de vivre*. We have never before seen a Hamlet who has in him such a subtle element of fun, or such an appreciation of the whimsical. Where other Hamlets scowl or snarl, Forbes Robertson only smiles; not a cynical, cruel, or sarcastic smile, but a smile that lights up his mobile face and seems to say to Rozencrantz and Guildenstern, "My dear fellows, you are both humbugs and fawning toadies, but I am too well-bred, too much of the Prince to snap at you"; or to Polonius, "I should uncommonly like you to know that you are boring me to tears; but still, you are an officer of the Court, a far older man than I am, so I must show my contempt for you with a smile instead of a sneer." There are frequent evidences of this buoyancy of nature united to a supreme courtesy of manner. In the scene where Polonius asks him what he is reading, and in the delivery of the well-known interpolated sentence in the scene with Polonius:

> *"It shall to the barber's with your beard.*
> *Prythee say on—he's for a jig, or a tale of bawdry,*
> *or—he sleeps!"*

in the memorable sentences about the camel and the weasel and "very like a whale" the new Hamlet does not show the slightest sign of irritability or contempt. His nature is too sweet to offend anyone, however much a toady or a bore, and he is too well-mannered to condescend to snappishness with his inferiors. This is why the new Hamlet was so beloved at the University, and so adored by the players. This vein of cheerfulness and humour, contrasting so admirably as it does with the serious and introspective side of Hamlet, is carried so far as the opening scene in the churchyard with the gravediggers who, we may remark in passing, are about the dullest and least humorous of delvers who ever joked in a grave. Most Hamlets approach this scene like mutes, and preach out their sentiment as if they were in a pulpit. Not so Forbes Robertson. His banter with the first gravedigger is in the very lightest vein, and without a doubt these constant waves of brightness and sunshine are of extreme value to the spectator. For ourselves, we never remember to have sat out the play of *Hamlet* with less effort, or, on the whole, more mental enjoyment. Many present, to judge by their enthusiasm and their rapt attention, could have sat it out from end to end all over again. Of how few Hamlets can such a thing be said?

We now come to the second salient feature of the new Hamlet, and that is the religious fervour that evidently underlies the half-distracted mind. We do not say that Hamlet poses as a sanctimonious prig or anything of that sort, but it is impossible to believe that he has not thought, and thought very deeply, of the "life to come," that he has not pondered in his own heart of "the dread of something after death," the "undiscovered country from whose bourn no traveller returns." On these solemn things, according to Forbes Robertson, Hamlet has thought very deeply, very earnestly, but with no suspicion of hypocritical cant. The mere touch with the supernatural accentuates these feelings, the communication with a spirit from the dead plays upon this sensitive nature as the wild wind on an Æolian harp, and it adds beauty and significance to the grand soliloquy on suicide and to countless passages that bring before Hamlet's mind the mysteries of the "unknown land." But if we wanted a pregnant example of Hamlet's philosophical pondering on the inevitable, and of Forbes Robertson's exquisite appreciation of it, we have it in one passage which the actor does not preach or grunt at Horatio, but delivers to him earnestly and confidentially and with that winning smile and the pure mind "half-way to heaven already," as much as to say, "Oh, dear friend, we all ought to think of these things." These are the words so beautifully spoken which convey what we call the religious undergrowth in the perplexed mind of Hamlet. They constitute, as we have ever thought, the loveliest passage in the play.

"Not a whit! We defy augury. There is a special Providence in the fall of a sparrow. If it be now, 'tis not to come; if it be not to come, it will be now; if it be not now, yet it will come; the readiness is all. Since no man has aught of what he leaves, what is't to leave betimes? Let be!"

And Forbes Robertson follows up this religious idea to the climax in the singularly beautiful death. Hamlet is wounded mortally, and totters feebly to the empty throne. We do not pause to inquire how the actor acquires that death pallor, but it is singularly effective. The finely chiselled face becomes rapt and inspired with a vision of the higher mystery. It is from the throne that Hamlet, weak, pale, and gazing on the golden gates of eternity, says:

> "*I cannot live to hear the news from England,*
> *But I do prophesy the election lights*
> *On Fortinbras; he has my dying voice;*
> *So tell him, with the occurrents, more and less,*
> *Which have solicited!*"

And then Hamlet, groping in vain for some "dear head" with feeble fingers, "the uncertain hand blindly searching for the dear head, and then finally closing on it with a sort of final adieu," and finding no sweet companion for his lonely journey, whispers, still gazing on some unseen seraphic vision, "The rest is silence," and then passes out alone into the unknown! But this is not all! The prince is dead upon the throne he never filled. Horatio places the empty crown on his dead companion's knees, and Fortinbras enters with his men, and all that is left of the dreamer and philosopher is "lifted on high by the shouldering crowd, on the battered boss of a shield." The contrast between death and life is admirable. The stage is no longer left as a slaughter-house of corpses, but as Shakespeare intended, with the majesty of death asserting itself against a background of martial splendour. "Take up the bodies! Go, bid the soldiers shoot!"

Photo: Barraud

H. Beerbohm Tree

H. Beerbohm Tree

We have spoken of the courtliness and grace of the new Hamlet, and alluded very strongly to the fact that the actor avoids all semblance of an irritability and petulance that might destroy his distinction and good breeding. But, at the same time, we are not blind to the fact that this consistently even tone on the part of Hamlet robs several scenes of their vigour and intensity. The pregnant passages with Ophelia and with the Queen mother, which were the strongest with Henry Irving, are the weakest with Forbes Robertson. We are not inclined to lay the blame, as some have already done, on the unpoetical influence of the Ophelia or the inexperience of the Gertrude. We ascribe it to the horror on the part of the actor, to the expression of that very irritability which is the first sign of worry and a bewildered brain. He thinks it undignified. But, if we are not allowed to see the King peeping from behind the arras where he is concealed, a crafty face instantly seen by Hamlet, but not seen at all by Ophelia, how can we account for the wild and whirling words of Hamlet, or for his change from a lover into a fury, now loving, now storming, now gentle, now furious? We maintain that Hamlet must be irritable, and even rude at times, to account for his "antic disposition." Why should he be so rash and explosive with Ophelia if he did not know, or were not convinced, that he was being tricked by the King and Polonius, and that Ophelia was a willing decoy duck? And if Hamlet's brain were not overstrained by the play scene, how could he possibly be so curt, direct, downright, and unfilial to his mother? No actor can get out of that. There are moments when Hamlet's beautiful nature is warring against itself, and those moments are strongly expressed in the scenes with Ophelia and Gertrude, and elsewhere. It will not do to stretch the point of courtesy so far as to suggest that Hamlet was not really in love with Ophelia, or angry with his mother, and that, on the whole, he loved Laertes better than Horatio. These thoughts certainly do occur to the mind in following the new Hamlet with all its variety, beauty, and charm.

With such a student-Hamlet, some of the omissions and suggestions are extraordinary. Forbes Robertson reverts to the old business of the two pictures embroidered on the arras or painted on the walls to explain, "Look here upon this picture, and on this," instead of the mental pictures which one would have thought would have commended themselves to such a scholar. But, strangest of all, he gives us the King's agonised prayer, "Oh, my offence is rank, it smells to Heaven," and omits that wonderful instance of Hamlet's irresolution, the sense of duty conquered by a kind heart, where he proposes to kill the King on his knees. "Now

I might do it pat; now he is praying, and now I'll do't!" Few Hamlets would omit that speech, and there is no reason for it, save a scenic change, which could be easily managed. The idea that Ophelia's mad scene occurs in a garden is pretty, but nothing comes of it. She does not gather the flowers and herbs from the flower-beds, but brings them in her lap, as of old, bound up with black net or crape. Neither the Ophelia nor the Gertrude are striking performances, but they will serve. Mrs. Patrick Campbell substitutes weariness for innocence, and indifference for love. The chord of youth is never struck. Her madness is very realistic, but it strikes the note of pain, not pity. Ophelia does not make us weep, but shudder. Her heart is not broken, she is cross, and too palpably forced upon Hamlet for a State purpose or a Court intrigue. We do not feel one beat of Ophelia's heart. Parting from the Prince, or crooning her wild snatches of song over the flowers, she does not draw one tear from the most sympathetic of natures. Claudius and Gertrude are too obviously dressed up. The one looks like the beautiful representative king of hearts on a pack of cards, and the other like Semiramide, or a new Cleopatra. They are both, as represented by H. Cooper Cliffe and Miss Granville, better by far than the Kings and Queens of old, but we are not convinced that the new idea of youth in sensualist and matron is of much advantage to the play as a whole. It was Wilson Barrett who introduced the conception with Mr. Willard and Miss Margaret Leighton, but the dire necessity for the alteration has never been clearly pointed out. The Horatio of Mr. Harrison Hunter was incomprehensible. What is the value to any Hamlet of an Horatio who is a prig, and a kind of overgrown Osric, an inanimate creature with no trace of sympathy or affection in his composition? Some Hamlets purposely select colourless Horatios because a good Horatio is too similar to Hamlet in temperament, and consequently detracts from the success of the Prince of Denmark. But Forbes Robertson is not an actor of that pattern, and knows that the better Horatio is played the better it is for Hamlet. But to counteract this we had an excellent Laertes in that sound and accomplished artist Bernard Gould, and the result was that the scene between Hamlet and Laertes at the grave was one of the best acted and most vigorous moments of the play. Here Hamlet awoke from the dreamer into the man of action, and the torrent of "rant," which was not rant at all, but the natural relief to an imprisoned nature, brought down the house. An excellent Polonius was found in Mr. J. H. Barnes, who was no senile dodderer, but a man who had been in earlier years a bit of a scholar and student himself, but who had the habitual tendency of old men to bore their juniors with reminiscences and old-world sentiments. Vanity, the root of most madness, had worked its will with the brain of Polonius. The Ghost of Ian Robertson was distinguished for its evenness of elocution and for its grim mystery of tone and idea. The Osric of Martin Harvey was just what it should be—perky, affected, and inoffensive; and it is seldom that the words of the player Queen are better spoken than by Miss Sidney Crowe, a clever and promising daughter of an accomplished mother.

Pinero's *Trelawny of the Wells* excites only moderate enthusiasm.

20th January, 1898

Pretty Rose Trelawny flounced out of the room in a passion, tamely followed by her humble friends, leaving Vice-Chancellor Sir William Gower and his sister "Trefalgy" glad and indignant, and his grandson, Arthur Gower, almost heart-broken. For a dangerous experiment in transplanting had been attempted, unsuccessfully. Rose, the pride of Bagnigge Wells Theatre—please pronounce it as "Bagnidge"—and reigning favourite of the district, had condescended to bestow her heart and crinoline upon the grandson of a mere Vice-Chancellor, one of those now extinct dodos of the Chancery Courts, who used to sit and administer fantastic rules of law under the name of Equity in stuffy hole-and-corner Courts near Chancery Lane. Sir William, though a fossil of the "much *obleeged*" period, and a vigorous old Philistine of the early 'sixties—a period when some of the noblest specimens could be found—had consented, strange to say, to an engagement, but imposed the condition, very reasonably, that before becoming a Gower Miss Trelawny of the "Wells" should spend some months acquiring English polish in the gloomy Cavendish Square mansion of the family. The process of acquiring polish is always painful; it necessarily involves friction, and Rose chafed under the friction. Cavendish Square reeked with "don'ts" and "must nots"—almost everything was tabooed as unladylike. She was even denied the society of her sweetheart, save when some dragon was present to preserve the proprieties; and, of course, all her old friends—those melancholy old tragedians the Telfers, the buffooning Colpoys, the merry, vulgar Avonia, the pert, genteel Imogen, the bilious, romantic Gadd, vainest of "juvenile leads," and the good-hearted general utility and unacted dramatist, Tom Wrench—could not even be mentioned. Minutes seemed months, days, years, to the pretty Bohemian in such an atmosphere.

Pent-up passion and intense ennui even paralysed Rose's love for her Arthur. Then came the inevitable rebellion. One night, very late on a very stormy night, some of her friends from the theatre came to call, and, as the testy Vice-Chancellor had gone to bed, Rose had them brought up to the drawing-room, where, alas! they behaved very badly, and made such a noise that old Sir William came down and frightened all save Rose into silence. She, however, gave a piece of her mind to everybody, and declared that the engagement was at an end, and that she was going back to her beloved "Wells" and her old life at the theatre.

Poor Rose! the month at Cavendish Square had given her a distaste for theatrical life, if not a taste for real. When she got back to the "Wells," she noticed, for the first time, "the smell of gas and oranges, and the hurry and noise and the dirt and the slang and the clownish joking at the 'Wells'." She lost heart in her work, unconsciously modified her style of acting, lost her popularity, and "got the sack" after a little while. Starvation or artificial-flower making threatened her, and she was without news of Arthur. He had gone on the stage in order to become a "Gipsy" like her, and win her heart again. One true friend she had, Tom Wrench, the ineffective actor and unacted dramatist, who tried to help her, and kept touch with Arthur, though, poor fellow, he really loved Rose himself. Fortune after a while ceased to frown. Tom had a chance of getting one of his plays, with a good part in it for Rose, produced, if he could find a "backer," and, after a little while, he found the "backer" in the last man in the world—the Vice-Chancellor. For Sir William paid a call on Rose, hoping to learn from her something about his grandson; and the humility and distress of the once haughty girl touched even his withered old heart, while the name of Kean, mentioned by her accidentally, awakened old memories of days when he was stage-struck. So old Sir William offered to find the money for production of Tom Wrench's piece. Tom was quite a schemer; he loved Rose; he was prepared to sacrifice himself for her happiness, and he believed that her happiness lay in marriage with Arthur Gower, a belief not, perhaps, well-founded; so, without warning Rose, Arthur, or Sir William, he engaged the young man for lead in the new piece. What a surprise for all three, when, at the call, Arthur presented himself upon the stage and found Rose there and also Sir William in a box! What could come of such a meeting but a wedding and—and what happened afterwards goodness knows!

A curious picture of life in the early 'sixties is presented by the ingenious play, which, if rather remarkably slight in subject, is wonderfully rich in quaint, comic detail; and the picture of life is the more fantastic because of the crinolines, Swiss belts, white stockings, beaded nets for hair, elastic-side boots, and other component parts of the ladies' costumes which only a lady or a Mr. Mantalini could describe. The piece may not present the author at his best, but everyone will be interested by his wonderful types of actors and touched by the tender human notes, used, alas! rather too sparingly in the play. One would need a column for criticism of the clever, numerous company, so I must pass by many who deserve praise. Mr. Paul Arthur's admirable work as Tom Wrench must be mentioned, and so, too, the brilliant if uneven Rose of Miss Irene Vanbrugh, as well as Mr. Dion Boucicault's clever Sir William, and the work of Miss Pattie Browne (who made her first appearance in England at this theatre five years ago in *The Amazons*), Miss Hilda Spong, and Mr. Du Maurier and Mr. Athol Forde, who has already taken hold of the Pinero method by having acted Dick Phenyl in the provinces. Mr. James Erskine, who is in everyday life the Earl of Rosslyn, plays the small part of Arthur Gower very cleverly indeed.

GEORGE ALEXANDER TACKLES SHAKESPEARE

In *Much Ado About Nothing* George Alexander sets his cap at Shakespeare.

16th February, 1898

As Mr. Lowell observed, or quoted, "The man who never makes a mistake will never make anything," and on this ground à *propos* of the recent production of *Much Ado* at the St. James's Theatre, I venture to think that Mr. George Alexander, as Pat Mulligan put it, "has a greater future before him than ever he had behind him." Could scenery, for the most part excellent, and sumptuous costumes of artistic design, contribute more than their fair share towards making a success, then, for what is lacking in the merits both of stage management and of acting, full compensation would have been made in this revival, which cannot fail to be compared by playgoers, those uncompromising "old hands," with a representation of the same play, not so very long ago, at another theatre. Such comparisons are, as we are aware, "odorous," and to be altogether avoided. That Mr. George Alexander looks the Benedick, "a young Lord of Padua," would be undeniable, if that unconfirmed bachelor were of the same age, or even younger than that other "young Lord of Padua," Signor Claudio, whom he disdainfully terms "Boy," just as do those two reverend seniors, Leonato, the father, and Antonio, uncle of Hero. Benedick, it may be fairly assumed, is older than the two Princes, Don Pedro and Don John, and, beyond all question, than Claudio. He is the link between the elders and the youths; he is Benedick in the very prime of his manhood, and fully eight years older than Beatrice, who had resolved to die an old maid unless she, like Benedick, should live to be married. In point of age, Beatrice is to Hero, as Benedick to Claudio. Beatrice is not a Miss Hoyden, nor is Benedick a "touch-and-go" Charles Harcourt; Miss Julia Neilson would be quite unfitted for Miss Hoyden, while Mr. Alexander carries in his face just so much of cynical expression as would make the character of the careless young roysterer quite unsuitable to him, though it ought to be a natural gift on which he should have traded when contemplating the part of Benedick. With another two months' careful study and intelligent rehearsal,

Mr. Alexander might have given us an ideal Benedick, and a perfectly stage-managed representation of the play, which, as it is, seems to justify its title of *Much Ado About Nothing*.

When Mr. Alexander comes to the serious dramatic situation where he breaks with the Prince and challenges Claudio, how excellent he is! He would have done well had he turned back and studied the character from this one standpoint. The two scenes in the garden, where, first, Benedick overhears Don Pedro, Claudio and Leonato talking about the love of Beatrice for him, and, secondly, where Beatrice (apparently in a sort of bathing costume) overhears the discourse of Hero and Margaret about the love of Benedick for her, show such a lack of resourceful stage-management as brings out all the glaring improbabilities of the situations, and thus reduces comedy to mere farce. The present arrangement may be supported by every sort of old-fashioned precedent and stage tradition, but Mr. Alexander would have done better had he determined to "reform it altogether."

Mr. Fred Terry is a merry Don Pedro, with just such princely dignity as is sufficient to mark the distinction of his rank. But how loud the three laugh and talk when Benedick has them in full view! How they "give themselves away" by the affected gravity of their exit!

Mr. Nutcombe Gould is a stately friar, a little too lavish of informal and eccentric blessings.

Miss Fay Davis seems to be thrown away on Hero, or Hero thrown away on Miss Fay Davis: a knotty point not to be decided off-hand. The low comic parts of clown Dogberry and pantaloon Verges are—well, I may here make a comparison, putting it in the form of a question, and asking if there be any playgoer who may remember being taken, when he was quite a boy, at a genuinely critical age, to see Keeley as Dogberry and Buckstone as Verges? Oh, the impenetrable stolid stupidity of that Dogberry! and the obsequious admiration of that deaf old Verges! *Passons*, Mr. W. H. Vernon is a noble and dignified Leonato, failing only once, and that is when, during "the chapel scene," he asks in a light-hearted way if anybody would oblige him with a sword, just to put an end to his life. And the Antonio of Mr. Beveridge is excellent, conveying the idea that he is a great traveller, and has just returned from a little tour in Ireland, where he has caught just the least taste in life of the brogue, and is ready at the shortest notice to whip out a shillelagh and cry "Wigs on the Green!" before Claudio and Don Pedro know where they are. Capital! In my 'umble opinion, it would be very difficult to find a better representative of that melodramatic villain, Don John, than is

Photo: *"The Theatre"*

Johnston Forbes-Robertson

Photo: Falk, New York

George Alexander in "Much Ado About Nothing"

Photo: Lizzie Caswell Smith

John Martin-Harvey

Photo: Lizzie Caswell Smith

Henry Ainley

Mr. H. B. Irving. But Oh, Mr. Irving, junior, beware of adding syllables and dropping the voice! beware of mannerism, for this Don John is but a twin brother to that part of a quite modern up-to-date villain wherein you so recently distinguished yourself, at this theatre, on these very boards! On the whole, the revival will excite curiosity, which will be allayed by the time the next novelty is ready for production.

NELLIE FARREN'S BENEFIT

Next "Our Nellie" takes her Benefit.

3rd March, 1898

With those magnificent English cheers volleying and thundering from roof to floor of dear old Drury; with one's ears ringing a medley of "Auld Lang Syne," "God Bless 'Our Nellie,'" and "God Save the Queen"; with hats thrown in the air, and a forest of handkerchiefs waved in every direction; with echoes of addresses and speeches and compliments of every kind; with the tuneful gallery boys taking up in unison every song that alluded to their pet; with the sight, never to be forgotten in a life-time, of this multitudinous sea of faces; and, perhaps best of all, with the beloved and pathetic accents of that dear familiar voice, "Thank ye, sir," it is honestly a difficult matter to write without emotion of the scene that took place yesterday within the walls of a theatre—a scene, we venture to think, that has never before been presented in any age or any history. We defy the oldest memory or the safest book of stage events to beat it as a record. Edmund Kean in this very theatre is supposed to have said, "The pit rose at me." But far more than the pit; every imaginable section of the house rose at Nellie Farren, a genius in a family which had a talent for producing them.

They say it is a good thing to begin at the beginning. On this occasion we have no intention of doing anything of the kind. We shall begin at the end, for superb and varied and exciting as the programme was, with "toys for all tastes," still the real fun and interest started when the sweet, gentle, and electric-lighted Ellaline Terriss came up a trap as a Fairy Queen and began "transforming" the characters in the good old-fashioned way. We doubt if the youngsters of to-day know the first meaning of a transformation scene. It means that the characters employed in the opening, the lover, his lass, the comic man, the old man, and so on are transformed into harlequin, columbine, pantaloon, and jolly old clown. If anyone cares to read the story of the Italian pantomime—that is to say, of the loves of Harlequin and Columbine—they will perceive how logical and complete the story and the method are. It did one's heart good to see such a harlequinade as was presented yesterday. When the transformation did come it was a revelation. We have had some experience in such matters. But not even in the days of Rosina Wright was such a Columbine seen on any English stage as Miss Letty Lind. She was a Whistlerian Columbine. She reversed the old process, and changed from white to black. The out-of-date tarlatan skirts were of dainty black tulle. The pink silk stockings were black. But, costume apart, Miss Letty Lind was as pretty as a picture and danced to perfection, with grace, abandon, and an indefinable charm that the old Italian school never gave. The audience, however tired or weary, would have liked to see that wild Whistlerian, Dudley Hardy columbine in many more scenes. And, as good luck would have it, the new-school columbine had an ideal harlequin in Willie Warde. He was grace personified. Milano and Fred Payne of old days would have owned the same. It was really worth all the money to see Letty Lind and Willie Warde dance. There is no mistaking art and taste. Fred Storey and Edmund Payne as pantaloon and clown kept "the pot a-bilin'," as the street boys used to say, and there is no need to ask about the fun of Arthur Roberts as the "bobbie," a character that has crept into the harlequinade in exchange for a not very interesting person called a "sprite," who at one time was supposed to be indispensable. The days of Grimaldi are days known to very few now alive. To have seen Edmund Kean or Grimaldi is a recollection indeed. But certainly the days of Madame Vestris and Flexmore were rivalled in talent and skill yesterday.

The harlequinade, undertaken by clever people, teemed with good things. We shall ever recall the Fleet Street newspaper boy of Tom Thorne; the singing swell of Huntley Wright; the soldier and Susannah of Will Bishop and Louie Freear; the two babes, in a double perambulator, of Eva Moore and H. V. Esmond, the crying of the one and the pathos of the other quite unequalled; the nurse of Susie Vaughan, and the street orator of Seymour Hicks, who started one of the very finest "rallies" ever seen on the pantomime stage. Harry Nicholls made up to perfection as a well-known character, here called "Rummun, the Restaurateur"; Harry Paulton, as a deaf-and-dumb man; and Edward Righton, a "Simple Simon, who met a pieman, going to the fair," all gave excellent assistance. But think of Phyllis Broughton, Katie Seymour, Madge Greet, Kitty Loftus, Marie Lloyd, Kate James, Topsey Sinden, and many more, all decked out as Seven Dials' damsels, and dancing round a piano-organ wound by H. de Lange, who looked as if he had stepped straight from Saffron Hill. Imagine Hayden Coffin, who knows his gallery audience, and makes them sing to his tune, together with Barton McGuckin and

Norman Salmond, standing round a street piano played by Lawrence Kellie. Conceive all the orchestra conductors in London: dear old Meyer Lutz with the beat, Ivan Caryll whacking a huge drum, and Jimmy Glover tinkling the triangles, all representing a German band, that wakes a London street from its propriety.

But we must hurry on to the actual reception that was awaited with such feverish anxiety. There had been tableaux and excerpts in costume from the best of the musical plays in London, all cheered to the echo; the Fairy Queen, Ellaline Terriss, had spoken her last pretty words in honour of the heroine of the afternoon; and at last the refractory curtain— it was very obstinate for a few minutes—rolled up and disclosed the scene of scenes in this eventful history. There was a huge dais uplifted from the stage, containing the merriest and prettiest faces in all London; the men were grouped at the foot of a kind of throne, where, with daffodil bouquets showered over her head by white-robed bridesmaids, sat "Our Nellie," in black, shimmering with bugles, and really looking as well as ever. She had as knights-in-attendance, or supporters as they are called in heraldry, Edward Terry and Charles Wyndham. It would take a volume to tell the notable people who surrounded her. Before the black-robed heroine, who could not resist the impulse to move with agitation and show the dear boys the "twinkling feet," was a huge album, splendidly bound, a present from the London Stereoscopic Company, containing the photographs and autographs of everyone who had contributed in any way to this record programme. Mr. Henry Hamilton's graceful, well-written, and heartfelt verses, distinguished alike for their style and finish, were admirably spoken by Mr. Edward Terry, who showed genuine feeling and had just the throb in the voice that was telling without being affected. As an old stage companion he was, of course, the very man to undertake the task, and he acquitted himself with great distinction. Mr. Charles Wyndham followed, at the inter-cession of "Our Nell," who nearly broke down at a very trying moment, but was supported by her clever, manly, and affectionate son, who promises to sustain the glories of the Farren family—the representative of still another generation. No need to mention with what skill and firmness Charles Wyndham spoke. He is as good an orator as he is an actor. He made the audience roar with laughter at the suggestion that he had no intention of saying much, as he was sure a good many of them wanted to go to bed, and he tactfully led up to what everyone wanted— one word or sentence from Nellie Farren. They hungered for just one sound of that voice of hers—that peculiar, well-known, beloved cockney voice, London in every timbre and fibre—and when it came it gave the mighty audience the first great thrill of the day. As she spoke there was a "silence that was felt," and when, in the never-to-be-forgotten accents of the street Arab, she smiled and said, "Thank ye, sir," tears rushed up unbidden to thousands of eager, loving eyes. It was pathos complete. The reaction came with an affectionate kiss from Edward Terry, her old and faithful comrade, and then the over-strained and excited audience moved out into the huge Drury Lane crowd, with genial songs, shouts of "God Bless our Nellie!" and anthems ringing in their ears.

Yet what a treat it would be to linger on the innumerable successes of this ever-to-be-remembered afternoon! The first strong one came with the famous duet from *The Forty Thieves*, sung by Kate Vaughan, who did not look more than twenty, with her old companion, E. W. Royce. Some of us leant back in our stalls, and as we heard the familiar words:

Oh! what a wicked young man you are!

time seemed to have stood still. There was Kate Vaughan, in Turkish trousers, with the well-known waving handkerchief which is her talisman, and there was "Teddy" Royce, apparently as well and strong as ever. Ellen Terry, as Ophelia, was a girl again, and she played the part with a weird sort of poetic madness, that has been intensified by thought and experience. But she was as ideal an Ophelia as she was—don't let us ask how many years ago—a Hero in *Much Ado About Nothing*, at the Haymarket, in the days of Walter Montgomery and Louisa Angel. Nor has time changed, but added to the power, of Sir Henry Irving, who gave the *Dream of Eugene Aram* just as he did on the Vaudeville stage, when he was determined to show that he was something better than Digby Grant and Chevenix, and Robert Redburn, but never dreamed then of Mathias, or Hamlet—possibly the best of our time—a performance that ought to be repeated for another generation. Lord Lytton's *Money*, always a safe card to play, but invariably abused by the "quidnuncs," brought out such favourites as Beerbohm Tree, John Hare, Charles Hawtrey, Lewis Waller, Lionel Brough, James Fernandez, Arthur Roberts, Evelyn Millard, Lottie Venne, and Mrs. Tree, but it was Mrs. John Wood, as Lady Franklin, who taught her companions how to get her voice and magical influence over the footlights at Old Drury.

The *Trial by Jury* was a triumph. Lady Bancroft, Ellen Terry, and others had seats close to the "associate author," and the jury surpassed themselves, instigated by that most excellent of judges, Rutland Barrington. Hayden Coffin, who anticipated the cheering with a Nellie

Farren verse in Tommy Atkins, and Marie Tempest, exquisitely dressed as the Jewel of Asia, were voted a delight, and we shall hear very much more of J. M. Barrie's bright little sketch, *A Platonic Friendship*, written for and charmingly acted by Winifred Emery and Cyril Maude.

But one does not know where to stop in enumerating all these wonderful successes. We should like to hear again the songs of Ben Davies, Miss Clara Butt, and Albert Chevalier, who was better than ever in *The Future Mrs. 'Awkins*. In fact, like the children after the fairy story, many would have said "Tell it us all over again." It was a day of days, to be marked with a white stone, those who were privileged to be present will never forget. There have been memorable benefits in our time—those of Charles Mathews, Benjamin Webster, Buckstone, Compton, and many more. But Nellie Farren—bless her!—heads the list this half-century.

MARTIN-HARVEY IN *THE ONLY WAY*

And now Martin-Harvey starts in management.

16th February, 1898

Success, absolute and indisputable, attended the opening of Mr. Martin Harvey's venture last evening. It was a first-night at the Lyceum, though not exactly a Lyceum first-night, for only Sir Henry Irving can invest that great function with its distinguishing attributes. But it was an interesting and attractive occasion nevertheless. A young and clever actor dared to make a bold bid in the foremost of our dramatic houses, and his brave spirit led him on to victory. An author of taste and judgment lent his aid by providing material that was at once sound, honest, and direct. Mr. Freeman Wills did not respond to the summons of the audience at the end of the play, and it was explained that modesty forbade. Let us hope that this was the true reason, for the writer has no reason to be ashamed of his work. He has taken a powerful and engrossing novel and planned from it a drama which is clear, distinct, and intelligible; which never loses itself in mysterious byways; which keeps to the high road of unembarrassed lucidity and successively passes the milestones of attention, interest, and success. *The Only Way* will bear compression. If there were moments when it flagged last evening the reason was to be found in the occasional wordiness of the dialogue, and a tendency on the part of the performers to "drag the time." This should presently disappear, and then the latest "drama of the tumbril" will settle down to a period of prosperity. Throughout the five acts not a dissentient note was heard, and, allowing for the friendliness of feeling inseparable from a first-night assembly, the enthusiasm exhibited rang out firm and true. We do not believe that an English audience will ever withhold its approval from sincere and legitimate work. *The Only Way* is necessarily a sad play, and a sad play, badly acted, is the surest and quickest road to disaster. That Mr. Martin Harvey succeeded is the more to his credit and to that of his faithful helpers.

As the moth hovers round a naked flame, so is the dramatist fascinated by the grim and gruesome story told in the most dread and dire chapter of French history. Revolution plays will be with us from time to time, so long as our stage endures. The possibilities are high, the interest keen and human, and the surroundings, built up by a practised hand, cannot fail to impart the needed touches of intensity and horror. Dion Boucicault dealt with the subject in an adaptation of Dumas' *Chevalier de la Maison Rouge*, and it was this fact, it is believed, which caused Ben Webster long to hesitate over the production of unlucky Watts Phillips's *Dead Heart*, which is now, by the way, exactly forty years old. Three members of the original cast remain—John Billington, Toole (the perruquier, Toupet), and Mrs. Alfred Mellon. It is an old story how the author learned with consternation that this excellent actress was to play Catherine Duval. In her own particular line he had the highest admiration for her, but this part was quite out of it. Apparently Miss Woolgar was of the same opinion, and only on threat of dismissal by the manager did she undertake a character which stands out as one of her most conspicuous and brilliant successes. A few months previously *A Tale of Two Cities* had begun to appear in serial form, and presently a fierce discussion arose, unkind persons asserting that Phillips had stolen his idea from Dickens, an accusation vigorously and loyally repudiated by Webster in a public manifesto, wherein he showed that *The Dead Heart* had been written and paid for years before *A Tale of Two Cities* was published. Over Carton's vicarious sacrifice much ink was shed. It was pointed out that Carlyle, and Lord Lytton in *Zanoni*, had a similar incident. But *The Dead Heart* lived and made a far greater stir in the dramatic world than Tom Taylor's adaptation of Dickens's novel given by Madame Celeste, when she had the Lyceum, in 1860. Here the late John Rouse played Jerry Cruncher, and we confess that, amidst the strain and stress of the tragic tale Mr. Freeman Wills presented last evening, we sadly missed the immortal— and immoral—odd man at Tellson's bank. Yet there was one actor at hand who could have pictured him to a nicety. We mean Mr. James Taylor—a most experienced and versatile comedian and character actor. The drawback to such a piece as *The Only Way* is the sustained gloom of the story, and our old friend, the humorous body-snatcher, must have proved highly acceptable. Jerry is a being outside the broad considerations of the French Revolution, but he is certainly not beyond the scheme of *A Tale of Two Cities*. In other directions let us remember that the late W. G. Wills and Mr. Kyrle Bellew have given us a Marat in *Ninon* and *Charlotte Corday* respectively, and that Mr. Joseph Hatton has shown Robespierre in *When Greek Meets Greek*. The old play, *The Black Doctor*, also deals with the Revolution, and will be remembered for the effect of a "multiple" scene, in which four different actions take place simultaneously.

Photo: Barraud

Lydia Thompson

Photo: copied by Howard M. King

Nellie Farren

Mr. Wills takes the love of the exiled St. Evrémonde for Lucie Manette, the ruthless vengeance of Ernest Defarge for the murder of his brother and the dishonour of his sister, and carries us, by a natural transition, from England to France, where the noble Carton makes his heroic exit for the sake of the woman he loves. With an excellent eye for contrast, the earlier scenes in London stand out in bold relief against the blood-stained orgies of the Parisian period. From peace we move on to turmoil, and when the author had finished with his opening acts the remaining ones were, to a large extent, certain to "play themselves." Hawes Craven's beautiful picture of Dr. Manette's garden in Soho carried our thoughts back a quarter of a century to the lovely rural scene at the Lyceum where, in the play of another Wills, Eugene Aram made the expiation of his sin. And the stage-management would have reflected no discredit upon Sir Henry Irving himself. The revolutionary tribunal, cold and merciless, swayed by conflicting waves of passion and indecision, struck upon the spectator with a fearsomeness which bore the best testimony to its dramatic force. Nor did the unsparing realism of the last grim act fail to impress the spectators into absorbed silence. Sidney Carton was no theatrical puppet. With his soft, sad face, lighted up by a new resolve and a new joy; a bright light in his eye, and a sweet hope in his heart, he compelled the tears of the house, and compelled them as much by his own power as by the appealing sentiment of the story. Mr. Harvey was careful, throughout the play, never to get out of his depth, and to our thinking the great virtue of his playing lay in his steady avoidance of any attempt to force a point. The Carton of the early scenes was a sufficiently emphasised "ne'er-do-weel," without being a raucous-voiced and shouting ruffian, as we have erstwhile seen him represented. He will have a better chance after the blue pencil has eliminated the unnecessary verbiage in the dialogue, and after Mr. Holbrook Blinn, perhaps fettered to some extent by fear of Lyceum "traditions," has more accurately gauged the pitch of the house. A character like Defarge must be "let go." We do not desire any Coghlan exhibition of "reserved force." Be it remembered that *The Only Way* is melodramatic in its very conception and essence, and that it never pays to mumble melodrama. Mr. Blinn did well, and was anxious not to overact. Only he and some other of the performers should not forget that the man at the back of the gallery is a person with rights which are not to be overlooked.

If there be any doubt on this point, let the players in *The Only Way* take guidance from that accomplished and ever welcome favourite, Miss Marriott. In her we saw one of the "old school"—the best Jeanie

Deans known to this generation, and an enterprising Hamlet long before Sarah Bernhardt thought of the melancholy Dane. "The Vengeance" gave her small opportunity, but she made the very most of it, and her musical notes were as true and penetrating as ever. A quite unexpected success was achieved by Miss de Silva in the part of Mimi—pretty, pathetic, and delightfully natural—while the veteran, Sam Johnson, lent breadth and significance to pompous Mr. Stryver. Mr. Taylor was not altogether too well placed as Lorry, but Mr. Tyars, in his common and congenial character of president of a court, was perfectly at home. Of Mr. Herbert Sleath it may fairly be said that he shows signs of improving in his work, and his Charles Darnay was fairly good. Mr. Fred Everill plays Dr. Manette with discretion, and Miss Grace Warner, though scarcely realising our ideas of Lucie, gave signs of careful training received from a clever and painstaking father. Most of the other people are simple sketches on the canvas, though valuable in the general scheme, and when *The Only Way* is rid of redundancies which will permit the dropping of the curtain at an earlier hour than twenty-five minutes to twelve, Londoners will go to see the latest version of *A Tale of Two Cities*. For it shows us that we have devoted young men springing up in our midst, and next to the repeated conquests of ripe experience nothing is more gratifying than the fragrant promise of youth.

LYDIA THOMPSON'S BENEFIT

DAILY TELEGRAPH, 1st *May*, 1899

Remembering that Lydia Thompson was not in touch with the present
generation of playgoers, that she had practically retired from the footlights
many years ago, and that to the very young she was known by reputation
only, the success of yesterday's performance was in every way as great
as could have been wished. The Nellie Farren benefit will remain supreme
and alone from the point of view of financial profit. Many circumstances
favoured that result. "Our Nellie" was stricken by illness when in the
prime of her powers, and there were enthusiastic thousands into whose
favour she had sung and danced her way. Lydia Thompson came back
to us as an echo of the past, from the "all alive" days of burlesque, which,
with deference to Mr. Gilbert, will, it is to be hoped, presently return
again. Memories of *The Forty Thieves* and *Blue Beard* were strong
yesterday, and more than one "old stager," of the practical order, came
on in the reception scene to hear Lydia say "Good-bye." Mr. John
Hollingshead, a living cyclopædia of information about actors and
actresses, pointed out a lady whom he described as the grandmother
of burlesque, and there were others—notably, Lady Bancroft and Miss
Kate Terry—who had not disdained extravanganza in earlier years.
But the audience was no less human than other audiences ever were and
ever will be, and the success of the Lydia Thompson farewell was, of
course, due to the enormous programme put forward, and the "gigantic
concatenation of talent" advertised for the occasion. A trifle tired, but still
enthusiastic, the patient pittites—and their brethren above—saw the stalls
slowly fill in the course of an afternoon which was surely overcharged
with entertainment. Fortunately several of the items were left out, but
as the "bill" played for five hours and a half, nobody was in the least
disposed to grumble. The revolutionary strains of the overture to
Robespierre denoted the commencement of the proceedings, and the only
drawback to enjoyment was the matinée hat—an abominable nuisance,
which some day or other will lead to an unpleasant scene. It was noted
with sadness yesterday that actresses are among the worst offenders. A
pleasant, condensed "melodrama"—no relation to an old friend *The*

87

Rosebud of Stinging Nettle Farm—introduced the younger Mr. George Grossmith, Mr. Huntley Wright, and little Mr. Edmund Payne, and to this succeeded individual "turns" by Mr. Walter Passmore, Miss Violet Cameron—who had a warm greeting and was in capital voice—Mr. Lewis Waller (still faithful to Kipling), and the Sisters Rorke, with a duologue from *Tom Cobb*. Another specimen of the same sort, played by Mr. Cosmo Stuart and Miss Marie Tempest, served as an agreeable vehicle for allowing the lady to sing a selection from *Carmen* and other tit-bits. Mr. Fred Terry recited an effective piece about an execution—more grim and real in its meaning than *My Lord Tom Noddy*; Mr. Courtice Pounds gave a Sullivan song; Miss Esther Palliser the "Jewel" scena from *Faust*; and Lady Bancroft delivered a humorous skit on people who go drinking waters at fashionable spas. *The First Night*, though a trifle long in such an extended programme, was humorously played by Mr. Tree, assisted by Mr. George Grossmith (with many facetious "gags"), funny little Mr. Robson, Mr. Hamilton Knight, and others. The performance of Miss Ellaline Terriss was very sweet and pretty, and it is interesting to remember that an old comrade of Lydia Thompson—Pauline Markham, to wit—made her first metropolitan appearance when she performed this character at the departed Queen's Theatre in 1867.

Mrs. Kendal recited a tale about a soldier laddie who had won the Victoria Cross, and showed motherly pride over what the newspapers had said about the gallant exploit; and then came Miss Edna May and Mr. Lawton, from *The Belle of New York*, with a sentimental solo and two whistling numbers respectively. The Americans were heartily received, and great merriment was anon provoked by the curious appearance of Mr. Charles Hawtrey as Cool in the third act of *London Assurance*. Here Mr. Cyril Maude made a distinct hit as Sir Harcourt Courtly, and Mr. Weedon Grossmith showed to advantage as Lady Gay Spanker's husband. Mr. Charles Wyndham, Mr. Fernandez, Mr. Waring, Miss Mary Moore, and Mrs. Langtry were the other principals; but these detached acts are never very entertaining. A monologue by Mr. Harry Paulton, less happy than some he has delivered aforetime, and a recitation by Mrs. Tree, preceded a dance by Miss Florence Levey, and then came a wait while the stage was prepared for what proved to be the most diverting item of the afternoon.

Upon the official announcement stood the names of Mr. Robb Harwood and Mr. Farren Soutar as joint authors. Neither of these gentlemen would probably be disposed to regard *Justice Nell* with an excess of paternal pride, for, to tell the truth, the object of the trifle was entirely unambitious, and possibly the absence of strict vigilance at rehearsal made it necessary that the voice of the prompter should be heard in the land— and, occasionally, heard all over the house. *Justice Nell* was, in fact, a convenient medium for bringing on in a mass a huge congregation of the prettiest and cleverest actresses in London. To quote the apt description of Beau Farintosh, the stage was, for the nonce, converted into a "huge parterre of beautiful flowers." The *cause célèbre* arose from an alleged assault, committed upon a bonnie fishwife, by a hulking and gigantic ruffian of a husband. This brute had used his Samson strength, according to the evidence tendered in his behalf, only after receiving severe provocation from a hard-boiled brick and an able-bodied coke-hammer, wielded by his timid and cowering spouse. When this shrinking and quiet creature turned out to be Miss Gladys Homfrey the house roared, but its laughter was nothing compared with that which burst forth when the wife-beating Anak was brought into court, safely secured with clanking chains. The precaution was a wise one, for the aggressive specimen of robust and tyrannical manhood was none other than Mr. Daniel Leno. The desperado wore a hat which brought tears into the eyes of all beholders, and voraciously consumed a basketful of provisions—with the contents of a porter bottle in attendance—introduced into the court-house by a fond and tender mother, whom everybody recognised as Miss M. A. Victor.

Great confusion was created at intervals by the prisoner in the dock falling out of it, and falling through it, but when he positively declared that he "did not know Mrs. Kelly," the gallery rose in its wrath and howled for his blood. "What, not know Mrs. Kelly?" asked "Justice Nell," whereupon Mr. Leno shed his last shred of truthfulness and swore that he had never heard the lady's name. To the "gagging" and "wheezes" of the inimitable Leno—who came out for the afternoon a combined Wyndham and Hawtrey in respect of veracity—the sketch was mainly indebted for its success. The people on the stage were kept in a state of merriment by the humours of the irrepressible Daniel—a Daniel who had come to judgment indeed, for after the President had interfered, and permitted him to depart without a stain on his character, the frail and fragile wife seized the monster by the collar and dragged him off amidst shrieks of laughter. Pit and gallery were delighted at this outcome of the trial. They felt that if Mr. Dan Leno had the audacity to avow ignorance of Mrs. Kelly, no fate could be too bad for him. But the laughter caused by the truly funny comedian had its counterpart of pure and genuine feeling in the overwhelming reception given to Nellie Farren. The sound of the familiar voice was music to the ears of the house, and, after the curtain had fallen, and she walked before the audience, quite sprightly and lively, the applause was tremendous. Not satisfied with a single recall, the "boys" insisted upon having "Justice Nell" out once more, and the Lydia Thompson matinée, if it did nothing else, served to encourage the hope that before long the famous Gaiety star may be again at work, amusing a public who hold her in high favour. Miss Compton and Miss Fanny Brough figured prominently in the sketch; a special welcome was accorded Meyer Lutz; and the authors were summoned in quite the orthodox fashion. As a novel departure from the orthodox fashion, nobody groaned at them.

Five o'clock had struck when the strains of "The Wedding March" were heard in the orchestra, as a prelude to the performance of a portion of Mr. Gilbert's whimsical conceit. The audience, tired with much acting and the oppressive atmosphere, rather failed to get the "hang" of the selection, but they were cordial in their applause of the principals, among whom were Mr. Lionel Brough, Mr. Rutland Barrington, Miss Annie Hughes, Miss Lottie Venne, and Mr. Paul Arthur. Mr. Edward Terry and Mr. Willie Edouin received emphatic compliments, and the guests—Lord Quex (Mr. John Hare), Lord Markham (Mr. Penley), Mr. Sydney Carton (Mr. Martin Harvey), Mr. Grundy (by himself), La Tosca (Mrs. Bernard Beere), Colonel Woodd (Mr. Edgar Bruce), Professor Jogram (Mr. J. H. Barnes), Colonel Sapt (Mr. W. H. Vernon), Lady Poor-Jo (Miss Jennie Lee), and Blanche de Nevers (Miss Kate Terry) —were gratefully recognised. Lydia Thompson, on coming on as the Marchioness of Market Harborough, was honoured with several rounds of applause. It was noticed that the quality of Miss Thompson's voice is still sweet and musical, and, although she has been on the stage since 1852, she is a young woman in manner and bearing. The two scenes from *The Wedding March* might judiciously have undergone some compression. But good humour continued till the end. Six o'clock was drawing on apace, and the particular feature of the day's proceedings was yet to come. Experience has shown that "receptions" are popular on these interesting occasions, and when the curtain drew up for the last time it revealed a crowded stage, whose occupants were "roped in" with festoons. Floral devices stood ranged about in profusion, and the cheers rang out in full volume as the Lyceum chief was seen leading the "lioness" of the afternoon down the centre.

Advancing to the front of the stage, Sir Henry Irving said: "This is not an occasion on which any words of mine can emphasise the heartiness of the manifestation made to-day, but I should like to say to Miss Thompson, my old friend Lydia Thompson—my friend and comrade— what a very great pleasure it is to us all, and especially to her old comrades, to take part in this demonstration of goodwill and regard. My friend Brough says, 'Hear, hear,' and I see upon his face a reminiscent smile, for he and I very well remember the time, before either of us had the honour of appearing before a Metropolitan audience, when we supported Lydia Thompson in one of those rollicking and tremendously successful burlesques of Burnand, who wrote so many famous ones, as you all know. I cannot assert that I exactly rollicked upon that occasion, but I know too well that my friend Brough did. I know that to my cost, I am sorry to say. But we both remember that the life and soul of that burlesque was Lydia Thompson, who has given to the world a wealth of gaiety, art, and accomplishment. We all rejoice to-day that she is reaping the reward of her work in the past, a very rich reward, not only in the treasurer's sense, but also in the troops of friends by whom she is surrounded, and who entertain for her feelings of affection and deep regard."

The French paid this country the extraordinary compliment of holding a matinée in honour of the English actress.

Paris Correspondent

While the streets were densely filled this afternoon with shouting crowds manifesting their sympathy with Marchand, a select assemblage gathered together in the Théâtre de la Porte Saint-Martin to make a demonstration in favour of English art, almost every theatre in Paris sent a contingent in order to affirm the solidarity of the histrionic profession, and the Lydia Thompson matinée proved for the thousandth time the anxiety of actors and actresses to co-operate in every good work. Truth compels me to say at once that the theatre was by no means full. Nor could it well be otherwise. There was, as I have said, the counter-attraction of Marchand in the street; while the weather was warm enough, for the first time this year, to tempt all but the most enthusiastic theatre-goers to seek the refreshing coolness of the racecourse in the Bois de Boulogne. The programme was simply magnificent, but, as it comprised no novelty of any kind, it was better adapted to country cousins than to those who live in Paris. Now, there is no suburban population here as there is around London to patronise theatrical entertainments, and this is not the season for provincials to visit the metropolis. However, the long programme had best speak for itself.

The proceedings began with the first act of *La Marraine*, which has just been revived at the Gymnase, and in which M. Huguenet presented his amusing caricature of the philanthropist who falls a victim to the seduction of the syren he sought to convert. Then came the last act of *Othello*, with the Mounet brothers as the Moor and Iago, and with Mlle. Lara as an ideal Desdemona. After a long interval the audience listened to M. Bartet, of the Opera, and to M. Coquelin *cadet*, who won boisterous applause for his humorous delivery of two of his most amusing monologues. The audience would willingly have heard him again and again, but it was time for Madame Sarah Bernhardt to appear in the becoming costume of the Prince of Denmark. She chose the scene between Hamlet and his mother, and she threw herself into the full force of her part as vigorously as though she had been warmed up to it by the preceding acts. The great actress has the immense advantage of being the youngest-looking Hamlet that has ever been seen on the stage. We are so used to see veteran tragedians in the rôle that we are apt to lose sight of the juvenility of the accomplished Prince, who was the mould of fashion and the glass of form, of the "Young Hamlet," who welcomes his college pals with juvenile ardour, and who finds in Ophelia's brother a foeman worthy of his steel. Madame Sarah Bernhardt makes none of the points to which tradition has accustomed us, but her Hamlet is from first to last intensely interesting, by reason of the earnestness with which she marks her frequently original reading of the part. After she had several times returned to the stage to bow her acknowledgments of the applause showered upon her, there was a terribly long wait, which was too much for the patience of even a French audience, but finally the curtain rose on the second act of M. Maurice Donnay's bold version of *Lysistrata*. The heroine is a character singularly well adapted to show all Madame Réjane's talents to the fullest advantage, and the clever comédienne revelled in all the audacious *sous entendus* of the witty dialogue. *Lysistrata* is by no means a play *pour les jeunes filles dont on coupe le pain en tartines*, but it is very cleverly written, and it was excellently acted by the troupe of the Vaudeville. The programme comprised more singing by artists of the Opera and Opéra-Comique, but the prodigious matinée was finally brought to a close by the second act of M. Rostand's *Cyrano de Bergerac*, with M. Coquelin, of course, in the personage of the long-nosed hero, a part which he has made his own. The receipts from the performance were between fifteen and twenty thousand francs.

A MIDSUMMER NIGHT'S DREAM

PALL MALL GAZETTE, 11th January, 1900

Mr. Tree's most recent achievement is in every sense notable; he has not only given us the finest production of Shakespeare's comedy, but in it he plays Bottom as certainly it has not been played by any actor since Phelps. For a manager, a great production, with all its enormous labour and profuse expenditure, *is*, if it be successful, in itself sufficient cause for triumph; but when the manager is actor too, and finds himself precisely fitted with the part best fitted to display his talent, the result is as legitimate an occasion of pride as when the general has to fight in person, and, like Napoleon at Lodi, himself carries the colours across the bridge. It is not often, we believe, the actor-manager at any theatre is seen at his best; meaning by that, in the part best suited to him. There is something in human nature, more particularly theatrical human nature, which constantly drives it out of the appointed course; Liston wants to play Hamlet, and no one can persuade Sothern he is not a romantic lover. Now Mr. Tree is a character-actor, and, probably, the best on the stage; character as dependent on observation, and not on passion or emotion, is the medium best fitted for the display of his talent. In Bottom the Weaver he gets precisely the chance desired; how he avails himself of it, with what richness, and yet delicacy, of humour, will be seen for many nights to come—would be willingly seen by us again and again.

Yet Mr. Tree, who has cast himself so perfectly, has in Miss Louie Freear as Puck made a grievous mistake. Miss Freear's notion of Puck is to make of him a sort of male Marchioness; it is, in fact, simply a domestic servant, whose head has been turned by reading dream-books, indulging in a series of *entrechats*, from kitchen to scullery. It is not even droll, it is merely common, and has no more to do with Shakespeare than would Mr. Dan Leno as Oberon. The clumsiness of it is, unfortunately, all the more apparent side by side with the grace and charm of Miss Julia Neilson's King of the Fairies. Her Oberon is truly regal, while the mere fact of her being a woman just differentiates it from humanity. For her singing no praise can be too high; there is a rich thrill in her tones that suggests some gorgeous Eastern bird. We have never

93

heard the bulbul, but if the bulbul could be taught to chant "I know a bank," and that the bank of the Tigris, we should imagine it very like Miss Neilson. As Titania, Mrs. Tree plays prettily, but is scarcely fairylike. It is a fairy from South Kensington, whose revels are limited to Queen's Gate, and whose rings are to be found in Kensington Gardens. Mrs. Tree gives one the notion that Titania has smart friends somewhere, and is only out in the wood because it happens for the time to be a society fad. Nor need even a fairy wear quite so fixed a smile; and its constancy makes one suspect the Fairy Queen's true amiability.

But in the general cast there are few blemishes. Of the quartet of lovers, always, to us, tedious, and surely capable of some compression, Miss Dorothea Baird's Helena is by far the most successful. Miss Baird will probably never make an actress, in the stereotyped sense of the word, but she is always seen with pleasure; just as there are some singers the *cognoscenti* tell us cannot sing, yet who are always preferable to many more highly cultured in the art. Miss Baird has a charm which is happiest in uncultivation; in Helena she manages to convey an impression, one understands better her running after Demetrius (very intelligently played by Mr. Gerald Lawrence) where other more gifted actresses would very likely fail. Miss Sarah Brooke's Hermia would be better— it very probably is—if one could do her the justice to get the *Mikado* out of one's head. But Miss Brooke so strongly recalls one of three little maids from school, that for our part, at any rate, we find it impossible. For Mr. Lewis Waller we can only say he was, unfortunately, so hoarse as to be well-nigh inaudible; later, no doubt, he will play the part as well as he plays most others. As Theseus, Mr. William Mollison was admirable; we cannot tell why, but we can always hear Mr. Mollison, whereas with most other actors we have to listen. We imagine the reason to be that Mr. Mollison is one of the few actors on the stage who have really learnt to speak; the others, for the most part, only talk. The "rude mechanicals" were without exception delightful; the Flute of Mr. Louis Calvert, the Starveling of Mr. Fisher White could not be improved upon; nor were the Snout of Mr. Percival Stevens, the Quince of Mr. Franklin McLeay, the Snug of Mr. E. M. Robson otherwise than excellent. One wishes to see them again at the end of the play. We feel, indeed, that the curtain should not fall on the fairies' stealing out of Theseus' palace after the revels, but on the cheerful yet subdued riot of the Pyramus and Thisbe company, finding their way out through the deserted great hall, after having been properly entertained at supper in the Royal servants' kitchen. After all, the true life of the comedy lies not so much in Oberon and Titania, Theseus and Hippolyta, or in the young lovers, as in the delicious humours of the "mechanicals," faithfully sketched—who can doubt it?—from some old Warwickshire friends of the immortal author. In any event, the curtain falls on one of the most delightful Shakespearean productions of our time.

ENTER HENRY AINLEY

Young Henry Ainley in *Paolo and Francesca*.

W EST M I N S T E R G A Z E T T E , *6th March*, 1902

Few productions are so interesting to the critic as that of *Paolo and Francesca*. For quite a long time the play has been before him in print, and he has had an opportunity of forming his own opinion as well as reading that of others as to its acting qualities; and the opinion of many critics of weight has been that it is superbly suited to the stage, unless, indeed, such observations as "It is a noble poem, largely for the reason that it is noble drama as well" mean no more than that it is noble drama to read and without reference to its acting qualities. There is no need to enter into a discussion as to whether a work unsuited or little suited for, but moderately suited to, actual presentation on the stage can be called "noble drama," because it is conceivable that under other circumstances than the available it might be rendered effectively, or because it may be considered as drama entirely without relation to its quality as a stage play. Last night, then, the critic had the opportunity of verifying the predictions of many who have alleged that this really lovely poem is dramatic in the normal sense of the word. The production gives Mr. Stephen Phillips all that he can reasonably desire; in some respects I think it is of unparalleled beauty so far as our stage is concerned. The dresses, designed by Mr. Percy Macquoid, appear to me, both in line and colour, the most beautiful, considered as a mass, that I have ever seen, and many individual costumes appeal irresistibly to the eye by perfect blending of lovely tones. Whether this is true to history or not is another matter; and though it is hardly the subject of this column, the question whether in pictures and fabrics the lovely colours that we see in mediæval work are not due to the influence of time rather than individual choice is not without interest. The ripping of a few threads of a doubled-down piece of exquisite antique brocade or velvet sometimes causes a disillusion, and induces one to wonder whether, in the olden times, what we now think delightful harmonies were not wild debauches of crude colour. Moreover, Mr. Telbin has painted some beautiful—and, fortunately, unobtrusively beautiful—scenery. Consequently there were often pictures that were quite fascinating. Mr. Percy Pitt has written incidental music rich in striking phrases, and his overture and *entr'actes*, so far as one can judge, are valuable pieces of music, rich in colour and strong in execution.

He has wisely made no attempt at what may be called local colour—
or, more accurately, colour in relation to period—for the object of the
music is to produce an effect upon the feelings of the audience and not a
suggestion of the music of the times, and his work, perhaps almost ultra-
modern in style, is the best calculated to affect those of the audience who
appreciate music at all. At the same time, I must hint that these remarks
do not apply to a ballad sung in the piece, which certainly should have
been set to some light and more or less obvious air in the old style and
not composed as if it were a passage in modern opera.

So Mr. Phillips's appeal to eye and ear was as amply fulfilled as any
reasonably reasonable poet could wish, and the acting, taking it all round,
leaves him nothing of which to complain, though in some individual
instances he has ground for grumbling. What, then, is the result of such a
production with this really beautiful poem? Disappointment. The play
is not really fit for the modern stage. One need not set up "Four bare
boards and a passion." I quote, no doubt incorrectly, from memory,
but one cannot help asking, since with such a production the play had so
little effect, what would have been its fate if it had been presented as
plays were twenty years ago? *Paolo and Francesca* doubtless is a dramatic
poem, certainly it is not a poetic drama. A play is none the more dramatic
for being in beautiful verse. Verse is an embellishment, not an essential,
and the noblest poetry in the world will not make a play effective for
the stage. Without going into the questions raised by Lamb's famous
essay, without pressing too strongly my private opinion that so far as
existing London audiences are concerned verse is a handicap, not a help,
I would insist upon the proposition that the piece, unless it would be
effective drama if written in decent prose, will not be effective drama
because written in beautiful poetry. What the people say in blank verse—
and some of them say it in such a fashion that it does not sound like blank
verse—could be said with a little mitigation of imagery in prose; and if
it were said in prose would *Paolo and Francesca* be an effective stage play?
For "effective," however disagreeable a term, is really a test word.
Every specimen of art must be judged according to the appropriate
method of its manifestation, and the play taken consequently in relation
to its power of moving the people who see it and not the people who
read it or have read it—though, indeed, the last may be taken into account
in cases, rare cases, where rhythm is properly insisted upon. Now,
although some individual passages and scenes were moving, the piece
itself did not move in either of two senses of the term; that is to say,
of having dramatic progress or of seizing the emotions of the spectator

and gradually intensifying them. Indeed, the most striking and poignant scenes were in the first act, which led many people, or everybody, to expect a great success. The note of doom was powerfully struck. Miss Elizabeth Robins in her description of the child-hunger of the barren widow has caused tears. We had seen the strong suggestion of the latent jealousy of the elderly man who, for political reasons, had married a beautiful girl and suddenly found the political reasons ridiculous because of an invasion of passion, and we had seen the two hapless lovers, innocent in thought, guilty in heart, spurred on by cruel fate to one another and to crime. And although blind Angela was not effective because the part was poorly played, the whole impression of the act was interesting and vigorous.

After this, however, there was no real growth. Duet after duet came and one almost wondered where the music was. The lovers met, the husband had jealousy scenes, the lovers met again, the husband unreasonably killed them, and there was an end of it, without, however, much more than a beginning of drama. One does not ask for violent effects; indeed, one would be well content with nothing more active than what was given, if it were less monotonous, less unstrange; for instance, in *Pelléas et Mélisande*, really a version of the same story, one could have been thrilled without the scenes most poignant in action, because of the curiosity of the atmosphere. There is no real strangeness in Mr. Phillips's play; there is no curious insight into character, no vivid delineation of the normal, and no hint of the unusual; in fact, of the strangeness without which there is no excellent beauty, concerning which Bacon wrote, there is really nothing. The piece moves from obvious scene to obvious scene, leaving the spectator without doubt, hesitation, or expectancy; without, indeed, really interesting him in the fate of the shadowy, rarely seen, lovers, who have very little together. One may, in truth, apply to them a criticism that applies to *Ulysses*, namely, that those technically called leading characters are too rarely in contact. One sees some battling by Paolo against the influence of Francesca, and none by her against his; but until the scene in the garden where they kiss there is little between them. In fact, there is a great deal more of Malatesta and Lucrezia than of the lovers of Rimini, and Lucrezia is rather too finely drawn for the stage. Presuming, perhaps rashly, that her first motive is a jealousy founded upon hopeless passion for the unlovely Giovanni, one must say that too little is done by the author to render this obvious and convincing. Miss Elizabeth Robins did all she could to develop it, and possibly a little more than she ought; and I am inclined to think that some of the reproach of melodramatic acting against her is due to her efforts to render clear the obscure. Certainly much in her performance was beautiful and touching; certainly, too, some was violent and restless; and yet one must recognise the fact that in every scene she was plunged, suddenly as it were, into the particular emotion exhibited by her. Moreover, speaking from the stage point of view, it may be said confidently that her expressions of affection in the last act for Francesca are phrased so as to seem a little ridiculous in actual utterance and are really unactable. This scene, indeed, clearly was difficult for Miss Millard, who up to then had played the part of Francesca beautifully, showing more than the others a sense of the music of the verse and acting with delightful repose. I could wish it had been possible for her, in and after this scene, not to have modified her method, but the modification was due to the method of the others. For Mr. Ainley, the Paolo—who, setting aside his unwillingness or inability to speak verse as verse, has acted very agreeably—became needlessly energetic. There is nothing in the last scene which need be declaimed by him as if he were addressing a mob, and if he would recollect that he is supposed to be speaking to Francesca and not shouting to an audience he would render it more dignified and beautiful. It is only fair to add that Mr. Ainley has a superb stage presence and valuable voice, and that when he has recognised the fact that Mr. Phillips did not write prose his work should be admirable; his gestures and movements are excellent. I hesitate to speak of the Giovanni of Mr. George Alexander. Those who know to some extent the prodigious burden cast on a manager by such a production are amazed by the fact that he can act at all, and do not expect that he will do justice to himself. Now Mr. Alexander's Giovanni has many good points: one sees a strong concept of character, one notices an anxiety to avoid extravaganza, but sees an unevenness of style and want of definition which soon will come. His Giovanni is powerful and interesting, but certainly less in merit than it will be in a few days. Mr. Swete pleased the house by an effective little piece of acting, and Miss Margaret Halstan played cleverly as the drug-seller's daughter. It remains to be said that *Paolo and Francesca*, if not the drama that we had hoped, though not expected, is an interesting, valuable production, and a noteworthy contribution on the part of Mr. Alexander to dramatic art. It is less moving than one had desired, yet it is so entirely lovely as a production and so unusually beautiful in its poetry that one may very well be thankful to have the opportunity of seeing it at the St. James's Theatre.

The grand revival of *The Merry Wives of Windsor* with Tree, Mrs. Kendal and Ellen Terry.

10th June, 1902

Falstaff died of love. The epilogue to *Henry IV, Part 2*, shows that Shakespeare intended him to play an active and important part in *Henry V*. But Elizabeth wanted to see Falstaff in love. This is, of course, only a tradition, but it is a tradition that accounts for much that is otherwise inexplicable. *The Merry Wives* is the only play the story of which is of Shakespeare's making. It is considerably the shortest of all his plays, and is, therefore, presumably the one that pleased him least. The scene is laid at Windsor, a town with which Elizabeth had more to do than Shakespeare. And surely nothing less than a Royal command can have induced Shakespeare to debilitate his greatest comic creation and the one in whom he took most joy. For Falstaff to be really in love was impossible, and Shakespeare's endeavour to meet Elizabeth's wishes in form, if not in spirit, resulted in a Falstaff so limited and reduced that he could not breathe the air of *Henry V*, and had nothing left him but to die. Yet even this calamity had its bright side. As if to compensate us for the loss of the true Falstaff we get a glimpse of the middle class such as Shakespeare gives us nowhere else, though it is common enough in Ben Jonson.

The play is a farce, and Mr. Tree treats it as such. In the course of a final reception, such as even, in his most sanguine moments, he can hardly have looked for, he made a short speech of thanks to the two distinguished strangers who had joined in the "revel." And "revel" was just the word. We may like his half-timbered houses and hollihocks, his inn with its ale-score publicly exposed, his oaken and old-world interiors, and his oaken and old-world glades better than we like some of the unauthorised cuddlings and cudgellings, the kicks and kisses that take place amid them. The piece written in a holiday, if enforced, humour is acted in a holiday, almost a Bank-holiday, humour. The five acts are reduced to three. This not unskilfully, Dr. Caius, Sir Hugh Evans, and the less essential characters being the chief sufferers. The chief characters are

Photo: Barraud

Mrs. Kendal

Photo: "The Theatre"

Mrs. Kendal

given entrances that Shakespeare never thought of. Anne Page—sweet, silent, and evasive, peer of Walton's Maudlin and Carroll's elder sister to Alice—passes without a word into her flower-girt home. Mistress Page and Mistress Ford gossip inaudibly together across the stage when Shakespeare still kept them in reserve. But what of it? There is a gale of recognition as Mrs. Tree pushes her way home between the hollihocks, and a hurricane as Mrs. Kendal and Miss Ellen Terry, silently confabulating, return from their walk. Falstaff swings in on a horse. What of that? He has, as we know, three horses, and the host of the Garter looks to come by them. All which, of course, is simply a cadging for so many receptions. But where is the curmudgeon who, in an easy-going play like this, will object to it? Here and there was some "mafficking" which in any other play of Shakespeare would be reprehensible. But why should not "the Merry Wives" be as merry as they can? There were, of course, exaggerations. Slender is not a man of parts. But the ultra-silly idiot, very cleverly indicated by Mr. Quartermaine, was a creature that Master Page would have sent about his business without a second thought. So, too, "mine host," most genially impersonated by Mr. Lionel Brough, would never have advanced the drunken Bardolph of Mr. Allen Thomas to the post of tapster. The whole thing was exaggerated. Mr. Tree's Falstaff is not new. Years ago two of our dramatic critics vindicated the dignity of their profession by controverting whether the tragedy of a big belly lay in its mobility or its immobility. Neither, as far as we remember, condescended to inquire whether a portentous stomach did in fact wobble or not. Mr. Tree makes a fine Falstaff. His make-up is perfection. He is hardly the man of breeding that the other plays require, but unctuous and raucous, chuckling and cuddling, with here a subjective gurgle of satisfaction and there an objective kick of disgust, he is the very man for the part. Yet, although he realised the physical enormity of the part, he hardly brings out the corresponding weight. He alights from the horse on which he enters with too much alacrity; he seats himself on benches that should give way without so much as a groan of timber, and he seems a balloon likely to soar where he should be a dead weight likely to touch bottom. But his is a fine performance. Mrs. Tree was a good Anne Page, though the enlargement of the part in the forest revels rather strained Shakespeare. Master Ford was admirably impersonated by Mr. Oscar Asche; he did his work intelligently, as became a Bensonian. Mr. Courtice Pounds was fairly good as Sir Hugh Evans, and Mr. Henry Kemble excellent as Dr. Caius. The actor made his character a real foreigner—a man that was not quite on terms with what was going on around him. What of Mistress Ford and Mistress Page? Well, neither quite condescended to the proper class. Mrs. Kendal was in her own way quietly excellent as Mrs. Ford. As Mrs. Page, Miss Ellen Terry was wonderful. She was nervous, and far from sure of her words. But when they failed her she gave their substance, and, which is not always the way with actors, her paraphrases showed that she grasped the meaning of her part. She was a delight, and anybody who wants to recapture the Ellen Terry of many years ago will do well to visit Her Majesty's. He will see more of the Ellen Terry that we all adore in Mistress Page than in any character that she has undertaken this last ten years. Neither she nor Mrs. Kendal quite accepts Shakespeare's level, but, taking the Merry Wives for something rather better than they were, both artists are delightful, and the opportunity of seeing them should not be missed by any genuine lover of the playhouse. But Miss Terry's playing was a joy, perhaps the greatest of the many joys that Mr. Tree has provided. He has done well, and has put his theatre ahead of any other for the Coronation season.

JEANNE GRANIER IN *LES DEUX ÉCOLES* AND *LA VEINE*

July, 1902

The welcome reappearance at the Garrick of Mlle. Jeanne Granier takes place in the comedies of M. Alfred Capus, of the best of which she is the original and ideal exponent. On this occasion the order of production last year observed is altered, *Les Deux Écoles* taking precedence of *La Veine*. Which is the sprightlier and livelier work remains in doubt. As both are to be given during Mlle. Granier's short visit, further opportunities of forming a judgment on what is, after all, not a very important question will be furnished. Upon its reproduction *Les Deux Écoles* vindicates its right to a foremost place among modern comedies. It may well owe something in the way of suggestion to the *Divorçons* of MM. Sardou and de Najde, the idea of a couple partly or wholly divorced effecting a reconciliation in a restaurant being common to the two. No such obligation on the part of the younger dramatist as involves a charge of plagiarism or, indeed, detracts in any respect from his originality, is imputed. In characterisation, moreover, as in story, the later work is the more skilful, and even in construction it may claim precedence. Barely a twelvemonth has elapsed since *Les Deux Écoles* was seen in London, and there is neither provocation nor need to dwell long upon its story. The two schools from which the title is derived are those of keeping the eyes always wide open and knowing when to close them. All men are scamps, says Mdme. Jouin to her married daughter, Henriette Maubrun, and the best way to deal with them is to shut your eyes to their delinquencies. Not at all of her mother's method of thinking is Henriette, and it must be confessed very assiduous processes of blinking would be necessary for her to remain in ignorance of her husband Edouard's infidelities.

Yesterday's performance is not to be compared with that of last year, when the piece was presented by the company of the Variétés, including MM. Brasseur, Guy, and Numès, Mdme. Marie Magnier, and Mlle. Lavallière. Mlle. Granier's companions constitute, however, an average travelling company, and comprise Mdme. Henriot as Mdme. Jouin,

Mlle. Marie Burty as Estelle, M. Louis Gauthier as Edouard, and M. Colombey as Le Hautois. For any deficiencies that might be noted in what is, after all, a creditable performance the brilliant impersonation of Henriette by Mlle. Granier more than compensated. Hers is, indeed, a masterpiece of comedy, admirable alike in humour and in finesse. Nothing could be finer than the yielding of Henriette to the old seductions, and the attempts to maintain a dignified reserve in the presence of her discarded husband and her prospective successor. Not the least of the charm consists in the animal spirits of the whole, and another attraction is found in the way the performance is brisked through, so unlike our recently adopted English plan of excessive deliberation or almost funereal slowness. A large and an eminently fashionable audience was attracted, and greeted Mlle. Granier with overflowing applause.

If—an improbable supposition—an English rendering should be attempted of *La Veine*, of M. Alfred Capus, in which Mlle. Jeanne Granier made, last night, at the Garrick Theatre, what we believe to be her first appearance in England, a title apt, if long, might be found for it in *Julius Cæsar*. That title would be *A Tide in the Affairs of Men*. Such a tide, Brutus holds, "when taken at the flood leads on to fortune." With this view, Julien Bréard, the hero of *La Veine*, concurs, and he sits patiently with folded arms in his office to wait its arrival. His optimistic creed is justified in his own case, and while he is seen or spoken of in the opening of the action as a penniless lawyer, overburdened with debts, he is in the second act making a rapid fortune, and in the third is a deputy, and in the way of becoming a Minister. His run of good luck, or "veine", however, scarcely lasts over more than two acts, and the conclusion of the play depicts a rather conventional lovers' quarrel, followed by a quite unconventional reconciliation.

Putting on one side the teaching, ethical or social, whichever it be, of *La Veine*, the story resolves itself into the love passages between Julien Bréard, the optimist in question, and his pretty and vivacious neighbour, Charlotte Lanier, a florist. While waiting for his chance, which no action or conduct of his own will accelerate or retard, Julien casts his eyes upon Charlotte and finds her fair. He invites her cheerily to spend three days with him at Le Havre, and Charlotte, though she protests vigorously against the frivolity and impropriety of his proposal, accepts. Quitting thenceforward her florist's shop, the business in which had been none too remunerative, she takes up her abode in the chambers of Julien, now her avowed lover. Little enough, except debts, have the pair on which to live. Indirectly, Charlotte is the means of bringing the awaited good fortune. Joséphine, one of the prettiest and most ambitious of her former shopgirls, has accepted the protection of Edmond Tourneur, a man of immense wealth, who is on the point of bringing a libel action against a newspaper. Mindful of old times, Joséphine induces her protector to trust the case to the lover of her former employer. So successful is Julien's conduct of the affair and so judicious the advice he gives that Tourneur is induced to trust him with all his important undertakings, and, in fact, makes him his agent. The tide has thus been taken at the flood, and the future of Julien is assured. "La veine" has done its work. Two more acts, however, are necessary in order to convert into a play what, as it stands, is only a historiette. These are found by the simple process of making Charlotte jealous. While staying with Tourneur at his villa in Trouville, Julien conceives a violent fancy for Simone Baudrin, a rich and ambitious woman, who sees in the rising politician a suitable husband. Vainly Julien strives to induce Charlotte to connive at his infidelity. Charlotte leaves, taking with her all his happiness and most of his good luck. Through the agency of Joséphine, the sundered lovers are reunited, and Julien, who realises the efforts Charlotte has made to fit herself for such a position, asks her to be his wife.

The scene of the play throughout the action is Bohemia, but it ends in the realms of respectability. *La Veine* seems to a certain extent intended as an answer to *Sapho*, and to show that what is called *le collage*, that is, permanent, if not recognised, relations between a man and a woman, may not be always attended with disaster. The play is, from an English standpoint, unedifying. It is scarcely, however, improper, and as a picture of existing conditions in France it is eminently truthful. Without being witty, it has a pleasant literary flavour. An admirable interpretation is afforded. No long time has elapsed since Mlle. Jeanne Granier, during some years the inheritor of the rôles of Mdme. Schneider, and the interpreter of the heroines of Offenbach and Hervé, came out as a comedienne, and she has already, by some half-dozen admirable impersonations, established herself as such. Charlotte Lanier is an instance of perfect interpretation, the character as designed by M. Capus being superbly realised. By this one impersonation Mlle. Jeanne Granier's reputation is already established in London, and her welcome is henceforward assured. With her comes the company of the Variétés by which the piece was first given on the 2nd April, 1901.

M. Lucien Guitry, who is well known in London as a companion of Mdme. Sarah Bernhardt, belongs now to the Théâtre Français, by which institution he is permitted to continue his representation of his original part of Julien Bréard. He acts with much power and feeling, though we are not sure that a more vivacious treatment of the part might not be desirable. M. Albert Brasseur is comic as Edmond Tourneur, and M. Guy excellent as Chantereau, a moneylender. In an interpretation praiseworthy throughout, the Simone Baudrin of Mdme. Andral was remarkably vivacious, and the Joséphine of Mdme. Eve Lavallière was pleasantly conspicuous. *La Veine* was received with much favour, and its performance may count as one of the most acceptable of recent French entertainments.

RÉJANE IN A ROUND OF PLAYS

And now Réjane, the actress I put next to Sarah Bernhardt.

1902

La Passerelle

After a lengthened absence from Paris, Madame Réjane has reappeared on the stage of the Vaudeville Theatre, to which she bids fair to restore its former popularity. Her *rentrée* has taken place in a new comedy by Madame Gresac, who, I believe, writes for the *Vie Parisienne*, under the name of Fred, and by M. de Croisset, whose altercation with a member of the *Figaro* staff has just formed the subject of a police case. The title of the piece, *La Passerelle*, is merely symbolical, suggesting the bridge between marriage and divorce, or divorce and marriage. The whole plot turns on Article 298 of the Code Napoléon, which forbids a divorced woman to marry a co-respondent. The article is peremptory, and there is no possibility of evading its restrictions if the accomplice of the lady is known. In the particular case of Hélène there is not the slightest doubt of her culpability, but her companion, having escaped in time, is unknown. The mere publication of the banns between him and Hélène would arouse the suspicions of the parties interested, and marriage would be impossible. Under these circumstances the family lawyer suggests that the Baron Roger de Gardannes, the gay Lothario in question, shall marry some other lady, poor as a matter of necessity and ugly for choice, so that the jealousy of Hélène may not be aroused, with the understanding that after a certain interval the formal marriage shall be followed by a divorce. The lawyer has the other lady at hand in the person of his goddaughter, Jacqueline, a woman of good family, but whose father was ruined, and who is delighted to have this opportunity of securing a handsome dowry without any risk.

It is evident that this sort of elaborate complication is very far-fetched, but it must be accepted blindly for the sake of the incidents to which it gives rise. Jacqueline has been living alone for a year in a villa on the Lake of Geneva, which she owes to the generosity of Roger, on whom she has not cast eyes since their wedding-day. When he suddenly appears at the villa, to which he goes in order to meet his lawyer, who is staying with Jacqueline, he finds to his surprise that the girl, who looked like an

107

ill-dressed German governess when he left her, has developed into an elegant and accomplished woman, and the expressions of endearment which he at first employs in order to throw dust in the eyes of the servants, who hail him as the master of the house, he afterwards uses in downright earnest. He has come to discuss the ways and means of a divorce, and Hélène, whose jealousy has prompted her to follow him, urges an immediate settlement of the details. The only ground for securing a divorce which satisfies all the parties interested is refusal of conjugal rights on the part of the wife, and the situation to which the adoption of this expedient gives rise is one that is more easily imagined than described. Enough that the rights are not refused, and that the official marriage between Jacqueline and Roger becomes a real union, to the complete satisfaction of both husband and wife.

The part of the heroine is fitted as closely as possible to Madame Réjane's measure, and displays all her comedy accomplishments to the fullest extent. A long scene at the very beginning of the first act, in which Jacqueline asks her godfather's advice about the professions that are open to a poor and unprotected female, was filled up by the talented actress with such an infinity of clever detail that its extreme length was scarcely perceived. Very clever, again, was the way in which Madame Réjane, by merely changing her coiffure and her costume in sight of the audience, managed to divest herself of her native chic, and to assume the portentous hideousness of a German governess. She was, of course, in her element in the dangerously suggestive situations to which I have merely alluded, and she danced among the eggs that metaphorically were strewn about her feet without breaking a single shell. Mdlle. Marcelle Lender was duly exuberant as the jealous Hélène, and Mdlle. Caron developed a sketch of an inquisitive lady's maid into a highly-finished miniature portrait. M. Dubosc in the difficult part of Roger, who, while being thoroughly comic, must remain the gentleman, was excellent, and M. Tarride, as the lawyer, completed an efficient cast.

Ma Cousine

What an amazingly witty writer this Henri Meilhac was. How, on occasion, the epigrams, the quaint conceits, the caustic allusions were wont to flow from his pen with the speed and force of a torrent of water. Parisian *aux bouts des ongles*, he thoroughly understood the little world wherein he lived, and which it was his great delight to satirise, exposing its littleness, its foibles, and its failings to the full blaze of sunlight. What an enormous loss the death of Meilhac occasioned to the French, and,

Photo: Barraud

Mr. and Mrs. Kendal in "Clancarty"

Photo: copied by Howard M. King

Réjane

Photo: copied by Howard M. King

Réjane

Photo: copied by Howard M. King

Réjane

incidentally, to the English, stage, all lovers of delicate wit and genial humour have long since realised. Oddly enough, some of his most attractive plays have failed to reach this country, or, at any rate, to become domiciled among us. There is, for instance, *Monsieur l'Abbé*, in which Madame Chaumont made an extraordinary success on the other side of the Channel, and to this category also belongs *Ma Cousine*, revived last night by Madame Réjane. So far as the latter is concerned, an intelligible reason is to be found in the fact that the piece is altogether too Parisian to lend itself readily to adaptation. Yet, in respect of comic intention and execution, it is a perfect gem. Of story it is well-nigh as innocent as the needy knife-grinder. But the absence of that particular quality passes almost unnoticed in view of the brilliancy of the dialogue and the dexterity with which the various scenes are manœuvred. Hardly a character is there, moreover, who is not modelled upon some familiar social type—a trifle exaggerated, if you will, but none the less amusing on that account. Who has not met with the amateur dramatist, inordinately proud of his first puerile effort and eager to declaim it to his friends; who does not know the self-conscious prig, puffed up with a sense of his own importance, who imagines that no woman can resist his charms; or the timid wife, carefully trained to accept her husband's slightest command as a law to be broken only at the risk of her domestic happiness? Add to these the big-hearted, kindly-natured actress, prepared to play the part of a good fairy, and by dint of her own powers of persuasion, to win back the recreant spouse to his rightful allegiance. These are the ingredients which go to the making of *Ma Cousine*, a piece delicate as gossamer and light as thistledown, but conceived in the truest spirit of comedy. To an English audience determined to dine on solid joints and stodgy pudding the play possibly may not appeal with the attractiveness it possesses for appetites less robust. Yet the gain is assuredly rather with the latter than the former.

Ma Cousine is Mdlle. Riquette, a celebrated actress, to whom Clotilde d'Harnay la Hutte comes for assistance in order to lure back to her side the Baron, her husband, whose attentions to Madame Valentine Champcourtier have become a trifle too marked. The Baronne brings with her a letter from a deceased uncle, who turns out to be none other than Riquette's father, although the relationship has never been publicly acknowledged. The result of the interview is a close and binding friendship between the two women. As it happens, M. Champcourtier has written a play, to be performed before the members of his club, and his chief ambition is that Riquette shall take part in it. To this the actress cheerfully consents, provided the piece is rehearsed, at any rate, at the Baronne's house. It would be hard to imagine anything brighter, livelier, or more adroit than the manner in which the author conducts this his first act, wherein he lays the groundwork of what is to follow. Throughout its entirety Madame Réjane does not for an instant quit the couch upon which she is resting, but the abandon, the movement, the vivacity of her acting suffers not the slightest diminution in consequence. The scene between Riquette and Champcourtier, he as anxious to read his play aloud as she is determined not to listen to it, is a thing of sheer delight. But it has its equal in that which follows. Riquette decides to write to La Hutte herself, hinting that she has fallen a victim to his charms, and that happily she has discovered means for making her way into his house. As Riquette pens the letter her own lover enters the room, and, glancing over her shoulder, observes the work upon which she is engaged. Maddened by his jealous suspicions, Raoul demands to be shown the note, and is eventually permitted to peruse it. Then all the woman's coquetry and cajolery are employed to allay his fears and to restore tranquillity to his mind. Madame Réjane is here altogether at her best; it would, in point of fact, be impossible to mention another actress who could bring to the scene such charm, such fascination, such certainty of touch. In the rehearsal that fills up the greater part of the second act Meilhac uses an exceedingly clever ruse, by virtue of which the action of the mimic play gradually merges into reality, each of the characters giving expression in dumb show to his or her true feelings. The device is a happy one, although obviously borrowed in some measure by the author from his own play *Frou-Frou*. Here, too, occasion is provided for the introduction of an imitation of the famous Grille-d'Egout dance, although, be it said, Madame Réjane last night availed herself of the opportunity with conspicuous discretion. Fortunately Meilhac in this instance reserved some of his most brilliant ideas for the last act, which, if anything, is even more vivacious and spontaneously droll than either of its predecessors.

The comedy, in short, fragile and somewhat thin in respect of story as it is, comes perilously close to being a masterpiece of its kind. It shows how out of the slenderest material a witty and ingenious author can manufacture an admirable evening's entertainment. It affords, moreover, an actress of Madame Réjane's calibre an exceptional chance of utilising her brilliant talents to the utmost. How thoroughly the opportunity was taken advantage of last night it would be superfluous to say. Nor could better support be wished for than that provided by M. Paulet, inimitably droll as Champcourtier, M. Gaston Dubosc as the Baron, M. Revel as Raoul, Madame Daynes Grassot as Madame Berlandet, and Madame Laure Surean as Madame Champcourtier.

L'Hirondelle

The skittish mother who is younger than her own daughter is the theme of *L'Hirondelle*, a comedy in three acts and four tableaux, by M. Dario Nicodemi, which was given by Mdme. Réjane at Terry's Theatre last night for the first time in England. It is not a well-constructed play; it belongs to the school neither of Scribe nor of Ibsen, and there is nothing whatever of Æschylean inevitableness about the progress of its scenes. It is more like a piece of everyday life in the loose method of its construction and in the quietness of its effects. But for all that, the play is interesting, and keeps the attention of the audience, though whether it would do so without an actress of Mdme. Réjane's talent and personality is greatly open to doubt. Finally, though it deals with risky subjects, it has a sort of a moral, and the young couple apparently live happily ever afterwards.

L'Hirondelle opens in one of those wonderful French lawyers' offices to which everyone seems to have access, and we are introduced to Mdlle. Madeleine Desnoyers and M. Lucien Lenoir, who make love in almost English fashion, perhaps because Madeleine is still being educated by an English governess. Lucien is something of a "waster," and does not appear to be doing anything for a living, on which account he is taken to task by his elder brother, a solemn lawyer, by name Horace Lenoir. But the younger turns the tables on the elder brother by asking him if he has always been true to his wife, and Horace is compelled to acknowledge that he is not perfect, and moreover, that his mistress is Sylvie Desnoyers, L'Hirondelle, the mother of Madeleine, whom Lucien wishes to marry. Here we have all the makings of a fine dramatic situation in the impossibility of such a connection between Lucien and Madeleine, and Horace and Sylvie, but the brothers Lenoir think little of it, and Lucien merely tells his brother how sad Mdme. Lenoir is, and that she "knows all." Sylvie then appears, and in spite of the fact that Horace is almost pledged to dine that evening with his wife, carries him off to dine with her at her cottage at Auteuil. In the second act the pair are discovered in the garden after dinner, and have a long scene of duologue, which would be dull were it not handled by Mdme. Réjane with the utmost skill. Mdme. Lenoir is listening in the road outside, a situation which goes perilously near farce. The second scene of the act is at the Lenoirs' house, and there Lucien, in spite of his exact knowledge of the relations existing between his brother, his sister-in-law, and Mdme. Desnoyers, asks Mdme. Lenoir to go and demand the hand of Madeleine from L'Hirondelle, a request that is extremely strange to English ideas. However, Mdme. Lenoir agrees to go, but before going she has a strong scene with her husband, which brings matters to a climax. The third act passes at Mdme. Desnoyers', and brings about the great scene between the two women, both of whom incidentally declare that the thought of losing Horace is killing them, and the only likely solution appears to be the suicide of one of the ladies. Mdme. Lenoir proposes on behalf of Lucien and her proposition is accepted. She then turns on Sylvie and demands that she shall give up Horace. Sylvie refuses, but finally is worked upon by an appeal in Madeleine's name, whose married life would be wrecked if a woman entered it as L'Hirondelle has entered that of Mdme. Lenoir, and for her daughter's sake she consents to give up her lover. Horace Lenoir enters at this moment, and is horrified at what he hears, but Mdme. Desnoyers is firm and dismisses him, after an effective scene. Madeleine, who has realised her mother's position, is comforted with the assurance that her mother will henceforward take up the rôle of Alice-sit-by-the-fire, and the curtain falls on the sorrowful remark by L'Hirondelle that her daughter has broken her wings.

The title-part suits Mdme. Réjane admirably, for it enables her to put forth her lightest comedy and also her intense pathos. In both phases she is brilliant in performance, and she avails herself of her opportunities to the fullest extent. Madeleine, the ingénue, is played with much charm by Mdme. Jane Bernou, who not only acts, but looks the part. Mdme. Lenoir is a tearful and crushed individual, in a monotonously low key, but Mdme. Suzanne Avril does all that can be done with her, and Mdme. Jeanne Bergé gives a clever little caricature of Miss Smithson, the English governess, who was nearer life than such parts usually are in France, being perhaps toned down for a London audience. The part of Horace Lenoir is rather contemptible, and it says much for M. Félix Huguenet's art that he contrived to make it natural and almost sympathetic. M. Pierre Magnier has little to do as Lucien Lenoir, the young lover, but he does that little well, and M. Bosman gives a clever sketch of the *huissier*. Mdme. Réjane is, of course, the bright particular star, but the acting was thoroughly good all round. The waits between the acts were again distressingly long, but had they been shorter, the play, which began at eight, would have been over before half-past ten. The piece is not a great one, and our English dramatic authors need fear no comparison with their colleagues across the Channel, but *L'Hirondelle* was heartily received, and provides Mdme. Réjane with numberless opportunities.

La Petite Marquise

"It's rather French, don't you think?" queried a lady in the crowd coming out of Terry's Theatre, after the performance of MM. Meilhac and Halévy's brilliant comedy, *La Petite Marquise*, last night. And rather French it certainly is. French in the easy sparkle of its dialogue—in the deft handling of its incident—in the frank artificiality of its atmosphere; above all, in the thinness of the moral ice over which it skims so smoothly to its highly moral dénouement. Unexpectedly moral dénouement might well be said, for in the first act husband and wife are so hopelessly (to all appearances) estranged, the complimentary lover so close at hand, that another end is only to be looked for. Moral, nevertheless, for husband and wife come together again, with the discomfited lover as an unwilling onlooker—though how long the reconciliation may be expected to last is another matter. The little Marquise may not be an altogether sympathetic character, to English ideas, but what a magnificent opportunity she gives to Madame Réjane for the display of her unique accomplishments. Whimsical, fantastic, even at moments ridiculous, though always fascinating, and above all, delightfully vulgar—*canaille*, if you will. What artistic vulgarity in her earlier references to her pedantic husband, in the fling of her skirt as she springs across the stage in pettish petulance; in the harsh thrust of her voice as she cries out in offended astonishment when, in the first act, her lover accepts his dismissal, and does not return as she expects. Or again, what a piece of declamation when she turns towards the women in the audience, and holds forth the same unheroic lover for their scorn. Nor are the other characters less ably upheld. M. Paulet, as the pedantic husband—an absurd, yet not unlovable character—who desires an imaginary entanglement with a real *bonne* as the most promising device with which the mutually-desired separation from his wife may be brought about, and who accordingly alternates between simulated orgies and researches into the history of the Troubadours, was almost convincing. To do more with such a part were flatly impossible.

So again, M. Félix Huguenet, as the exceedingly adipose and not attractive lover, whose ardour is changed to hesitation, when the Marquise, to whom he has so ardently protested, arrives at his rural abode with the news that she is free and ready to throw herself into his arms, is ridiculously life-like. The actors and actresses with smaller parts to play were—as, indeed, is more commonly the case in France than in this country—one and all extremely competent, M. Bosman's facial pantomime in the part of a footman being especially worthy of notice. The play was preceded by *L'Ecuyère*, a piece in one act, adapted from the German by M. Dormic. It sets forth the plot devised by an amorous young Marquis of the conventional type, whereby he may obtain an interview with a fascinating circus-girl—a plot which, owing to the blundering of a well-meaning friend, admirably played by M. Barré, ends in his discomfiture—and in the downfall of his matrimonial designs upon the fortune of the Countess de Noharmond. It is slight, though sufficiently amusing of its kind. Madame Suzanne Avril gave a clever rendering of the Countess who is mistaken for the circus-rider.

La Rafale

When a squall strikes the waters there is wreckage: that is the meaning of *La Rafale*. Apparently the life of Helene is peaceful and monotonous. She is ill-mated to a nonentity. She has unbeknown to the world a lover. She is happy. Then the squall suddenly arises. Her lover, a man of high breeding but given to gambling, announces that he is ruined; that he has in one night lost £25,000; that he has spent other people's money at the table. The outcome is disgrace, and, unless he can make good his defalcation on the next day, prison. Before the disaster comes he protests that they shall part. She absolutely refuses; she beseeches; she threatens. He is the best part of her life. At all costs she will save him. She is ready to sell her jewels, but, oddly enough, her jeweller cannot raise so large a sum. She then confesses herself to her father, and has a terrible scene with him, but the old man—a typical Parisian of the newest Republican upstart type—is adamant. There is still one way open. In years gone by she has refused her cousin, a wealthy, prosy, hard-headed man. He will help. He will pay the Grand Prix for virtue, but his condition—the woman. In her agony, where all efforts have failed and the lover stands before the hour of reckoning, she submits to the ordeal and the buyer pays the Grand Prix without demur. Then she hurries back to the rooms of her lover with a fine tale of how she got the money and a pocket-book crammed with banknotes, but no sooner has she entered his study than a shot reveals the tragedy. A woman has been sacrificed in vain. From the point of view of insular morality this play is of course to be condemned. It is sordid. It causes the heart to ache. It is cruel. But the work of art must not be judged by narrow standards. It is not the point whether the play is simple or repellent. The point is whether the author has carved from life a slice which is worthy of our thought and attention, and whether he has treated it with dignity. Now, as a cosmopolitan and a catholic in art, I have no hesitation in saying that M. Henri Bernstein, the young author who, on the right side of thirty, has already become famous, has treated a great theme in a very lofty manner. Mind, we are not talking of an English play now, nor of English conceptions of life. We are dealing with the life that Paris lives. With manners that are essentially Parisian. With conditions into which we must try to penetrate without bias. The woman has a lover. For him she lays down that which is dearer than life itself—her honour—and when she has done so it is all in vain. If it had been written by an ancient Greek we should have spoken of the grandeur of tragedy. Written, as it is, by a modern Frenchman, we are perhaps inclined to give him the lesser praise that he is a man who understands his time. It is a question well worth pondering over, for it touches the root of the French institution of marriage. The negative position of the married woman; the terrible spirit of mercenariness which pervades the Parisian middle classes. Bernstein is evidently a writer with a purpose, and his tendencies are of a highly socialistic aim. He derides the bourgeois, to whom money is a god, and he has some reverence for the man who, in the game of life, loses and pays the cost as one does when nature is noble. *La Rafale* is neither a play for girls nor for grown-up children who use the theatre as a dormitory of digestiveness. It is a play that goes into the marrow of one's bones, and would inspire volumes, instead of a short article. There are flaws of over-drawing; of one-sidedness; especially in the character of Helene's father, who is bereft of all humanity; but it is a remarkable work, written in French that not merely sounds as music, but is symphonic by the exquisite chasing of expression. Such plays, which overwhelm both the intellect and the emotion of the hearer, explain why the French stage ranks so high. Even without Réjane it would have deeply impressed the audience, but with Réjane and an actor like Pierre Magnier it creates an unspeakable sensation. Latterly in lighter work Réjane has not always lived up to her greatness. She has been apt to be playful and to commit lapses of taste as if she did not place high value on the understanding of English spectators. But by *La Rafale* she has with one stroke erased such reminiscences. She is truly great in the grandest sense of the word. She gives the woman in love, the woman in anguish, the woman in agony in such unmistakable accents of sincerity that it is not she alone who is struck by the squall. We suffer and sorrow with her. She sends us hence charged with thought and emotion.

Divorçons

Mme. Réjane is bringing her season to a close with three performances of *Divorçons*. The first took place last night, the second and third will be given this afternoon and evening. This very amusing and somewhat daring piece she played in London on the occasion of, we think, her last visit, when it was noticed at length. It is well known in French, and it has not only been adapted more than once, but has inspired several "new and original" English farces. Its ingenuity and brilliant and aggressive dialogue have, however, been unapproached in any of its derivatives. The piece is really acute comedy rather than farce, but as so often happens with comedies that fall just short of the classical, it has come to be treated as farce. Mme. Réjane's Cyprienne is a wonderfully animated and pungent impersonation: for some tastes rather too pungent. The spectacle of a drunken woman is never very pleasant, and Mme. Réjane's Cyprienne now seems to take a glass or two more of wine than was her wont but a few years back. The ridiculous tame-cat and victim, Adhemar, as played last night by M. Paulet, was so ridiculous that it was a reflection on Cyprienne's common sense that she should for a moment have thought of him as a lover. M. Chautard as Des Prunelles, the husband who brings the wife, bitter with the idea of divorce, to her senses, was of the three principal actors the one who clowned least and best preserved the gay, light tone of the comedy. A crowded audience was kept thoroughly amused. The comments of the Press on Mme. Réjane's unpunctuality seem to have borne fruit. Last night she kept her appointment to the minute, and, the intervals being of conscionable duration, the play was over before half-past ten. We do not know of an audience being released so early since a first-night a dozen or more years since at the Shaftesbury, when it showed resentment at the shortness of the entertainment. Last night's audience showed none; it went home with a broad smile.

Décoré

For her second venture at the new French Theatre in London, Mdme. Réjane has chosen a character of which she was the original exponent. *Décoré*, a three-act piece of M. Henri Meilhac, written without the aid of his customary collaborator, Ludovic Halévy, was produced at the Variétés on the 17th January, 1888. It is a characteristically sly, witty, extravagant, and Parisian piece, with which the author was held to pose as candidate for the place in the ranks of the Académie Française, vacated by the death of Eugène Labiche, an honour which was conferred upon him in this year. So exquisitely comic was it in story and character that

Photo : Walery

Marie Tempest in "Dorothy"

Photo: Barraud

Charles Wyndham and Mary Moore in "David Garrick"

it almost passed over the heads of the first-night's public, quick of apprehension as that is supposed to be. The wit of the dialogue and the acting of Mdme. Réjane, which certainly did not err on the side of reticence, soon conquered the public, and the piece, after obtaining one hundred and twenty-odd representations, passed into the general répertoire of the actress.

Its story is not easily told. Immediately after a brief honeymoon, Mdme. Henriette Colineau becomes the object of pressing attention on the part of the Parisian gallants. So eager in pursuit is one of these, Edouard d'Andrésis, that Henriette, after forbidding him her house, thinks it wise to fortify herself against his seductions by informing her husband of his persistency. Unfortunately, Colineau, wholly occupied with his own love affairs, disregards the implied confession of weakness and while following to Macon, on the Marseilles route, an engaging and fascinating Roman Countess sends his wife on the line to Normandy. Hither she is followed by the faithful Edouard, whose pleading becomes too eloquent to be resisted. All that a lover could ask would be granted, but Edouard has the mania of saving life when he should be following up his love-suit. After he has plunged into the water in his clothes to fish out a drowning man, and then saved, with the aid of an umbrella, an African prince from a lion, he receives by telegraphic dispatch the news that he is *décoré*. Unfortunately, in consequence of his companionship

(Even more unfortunately the cutting breaks off here.)

THE MARRIAGE OF KITTY

At last Marie Tempest puts in her provocative, enchanting little nose.

In French the play is called *La Passerelle*, in English *The Marriage of Kitty*. The two titles mark the difference to a nicety. Literally, *La Passerelle* means the little railway bridge 'twixt the up and down platforms; metaphorically, but in no flattering sense, it refers to a woman who has been coaxed into a kind of transitory marriage of convenience, in order to fulfil the conditions of a will. For the *pro forma* husband would have lost his uncle's fortune if he had married a widow or the Peruvian lady of whom he is enamoured. The position is awkward, but the family solicitor knows the way out of it. He has a fair ward on his hands who is sorely in need of a living, and to her, marriage—albeit, merely in name and *pro tem.*—is salvation. She accepts, and as she goes through the farcical form she decides firmly to win her husband's heart while gently clinging to his hand.

Whether in England such a game of collusion, aided and abetted, forsooth, by a solicitor, would pass muster before the Court of Sir Francis Jeune, the Queen's Proctor, and the Incorporated Law Society, I will leave undiscussed. Nor need one pause to inquire into other legal delicacies connected with the peculiar case of Kitty's nominal matrimony. For this is farcical comedy, and in that benighted region the improbable is acceptable provided that it is amusing. Now, to a great extent the play, which Mr. Cosmo Gordon Lennox has distilled with infinite pains out of very slippery French material, is highly entertaining. And if the third act were but a pointed end to a good story, the whole evening would have been one of boundless merriment; but unfortunately after the second act, which culminates in the climax of "he fell in love with his wife," there is no more to be said. We are absorbed in Kitty and her husband; what becomes of her hysterical Peruvian rival does not interest us; and to devote a whole act to needless explanation and disentanglement is like spoiling the effect of an excellent champagne dinner by a wanton surfeit of whisky and soda. Nor do I see how Mr. Lennox can mend matters except by vigorous pruning. The act is superfluous, and the more it is reduced the better it will be for the ultimate success of the play.

After this objection, which applies to many farcical comedies, Mr. Lennox may be complimented on having done his difficult task with much skill and taste. Strictly speaking, the drift of the play is towards thin ice and shallow waters, but Mr. Lennox has so neatly veneered all that might offend Mrs. Grundy, he has made the problem of the wife's conquest so attractive, that one forgives all undercurrents for the sake of the pretty wit that rules supreme.

The Marriage of Kitty is one of those plays which are made or marred by an actress. It will be a great success because Miss Marie Tempest has grasped every phase of the part and has endowed it with all the captivation of her personality and intellect. She is loyally supported and stimulated by Mr. Leonard Boyne, somewhat weighty as a comedian, but a magnetic player and the finest stage lover of the younger generation; by Miss Ellis Jeffreys, always elegant, always refined, even when she has to impersonate such a hazardous character as that of the hysterical South American; by Mr. Lloyd Lowndes and Miss Elsie Chester, both characteristic in the miniature parts of valet and *femme de chambre*.

But, after all, Miss Marie Tempest is the play, and her acting is the one subject that occupies our thoughts after the curtain's fall. For we have here the manifestation of something novel: an English actress exhibiting all the most salient qualities of a Parisian *comédienne*. Whether by intuition or by study, Miss Tempest has learned to understand the intrinsic meaning of the French saying, *Glissez, n'appuyez pas*—insinuate, don't insist; and thus without apparent effort, without boisterousness or emphasis, she keeps her audience in a state of fascination and gentle glee. It is an art of wonderful subtlety and refinement. It is, in fact, the art of comedy, which so many of our actors confound with the mere craft of farce.

CRICHTON IN LONDON AND PARIS

Concerning *The Admirable Crichton* I choose an account of the one-night performance given in Paris. It is the *Daily Telegraph's* special correspondent writing. The play was first produced in London at the Duke of York's Theatre on 4th November, 1902.

People are asking this evening why Mr. Charles Frohman should have taken all the trouble and incurred such great expense to present Mr. J. M. Barrie's fantasy, *The Admirable Crichton*, for one night only, when the indications promised a week at least of sustained success. At all events, the seats were at a premium to-day, and the French journalists, at first a little indifferent to the visit of the Duke of York's Theatre company, waxed impatient to interview Mr. Frohman and his managers upon the possible permanent outcome of the venture. Nothing untoward has attended the preparations, but then, Mr. Dion Boucicault, with Mr. Macrae on the one hand and Mr. Hamilton and Mr. Matthews on the other, have left nothing to chance. The quartette of management before and behind the curtain have been indefatigable, and have, I should say, had very little sleep since leaving London, and the prospect of recovering arrears of rest before Tuesday night is exceeding remote. On the arrival of the company there was the task of quartering them at several hotels, the night of the Grand Prix bringing an enormous demand for accommodation. That every lady and gentleman should have found no reason for dissatisfaction is something in itself.

Certainly, in spite of the grey, variable day, the few hours of leisure which the principals have enjoyed were particularly pleasant. I am not disclosing private affairs unduly when I say that Mr. H. B. Irving spent the forenoon in adding to his store of knowledge of criminal jurisprudence—a subject which, as an author, he has made his own—and I esteemed it a privilege to pass the morning with him at the Palais de Justice and in the police-courts. At the Théâtre de la Renaissance the stage-hands had snatched a couple of hours of rest at 4 A.M. before resuming. Mr. Dion Boucicault arrived with his special goods train from Boulogne at nine o'clock last night, and no time was lost in transferring from the Gare du Nord the scenery and properties to great trucks in waiting. An hour and a quarter were occupied in this work, but it was not until one o'clock this morning that the last piece of painted canvas was inside the theatre. The Renaissance is a sort of inverted Criterion, for one has to ascend three flights before the level of the stage is reached. This means that every bit of scenery had to be hauled up by pulley thirty feet from the street before it could be pushed into the narrow opening leading to the scene dock. A greater obstacle to rapidity of working could not be devised. However, British energy overcame it. The stage, although some feet less in depth than that of the Duke of York's Theatre, has a proscenium opening two feet wider. I have heard the stage compared to both Blackpool and Glasgow.

All the morning the carpenters and electricians were busy. Electricity plays an unsuspected part. For instance, when the Admirable Crichton, upon the island, reduces his future but temporary subjects to subordination, it is the fragrant steam of his cooking cauldron which proves irresistible to the hungry aristocrats. This steam is supposed to blow in the direction they have taken, and from which, as the appetising aroma reaches them, they one by one slip back to sit in a circle around the camp fire, thus surrendering the superiority conferred upon them by the accident of birth, which proves of no value away from the resources of civilisation. The steam actually does blow in the desired direction. That effect is produced by a small electric motor which, at the same time, agitates the strips of red silk, marvellously representing flames beneath the pot. Real fire was forbidden by the London County Council, hence this original device.

The removal of the scenery on its return journey to London virtually began at the close of the second act, the first set being required at the end of the play a second time. The audience was unaware that before the curtain fell the exterior view of the hut on the island, with the false stage imitating irregularities of ground, were already on their way to the railroad, having been lowered into the street directly they were no longer wanted. The interior of the hut, with its electrical fittings, promptly followed. Three hours remained after midnight to convey the rest of the impedimenta to the Gare du Nord and to load up the trucks, the special to Boulogne being timed to start at 3 A.M. on Tuesday in order that a specially chartered cargo steamer might receive the goods and cross the Straits to Folkestone. This steamer should arrive early enough to permit the scenery getting back to town in readiness for Tuesday evening's performance at the Duke of York's Theatre. If it does not, then there will be much disappointment, for I hear that the bookings are very heavy, notwithstanding the prolonged run of the piece. The principals, company, staff, and stage hands all leave Paris at 8.30.

What did Paris think of *The Admirable Crichton*? The brilliant and full house which witnessed the unique performance to-night at the Renaissance was mostly Anglo-Saxon. For one word spoken in French, in boxes or corridors, between the acts there were ten uttered in English. The French minority present thought it sounded so lively and bright to hear clear English voices speaking in a bell-like intonation which, Parisians said, gave quite a different impression from that of a French crowd. The few Parisians who were in the audience, however, were representative. There were many of those members of the French aristocracy who always spend a portion of the season in London. The stage was very well represented, among the actors of the Comédie Française being M. le Bargy, with his wife, who acts in other theatres. M. Jules Claretie went behind the scenes for some moments. The Paris Press was fairly well to the fore, but the chief critics had not attended, because hardly one of them could have understood the dialogue. Of the British and American colonies, all the best-known members were present. Sir Edmund Monson sat in the State box to the right of the audience, Lady Monson being unfortunately prevented from attending, by illness. The American Embassy had a box, in which not a seat was vacant.

To mention a few among the other spectators, M. Octave Uzanne, the art critic and littérateur, had come in his capacity as translator of the play, which he is engaged in adapting into French. Mrs. Barrie was in the audience, but the author had been unable to attend. I noticed in the passages talking animatedly between the acts Mr. William Gillette, who will act in *The Admirable Crichton* in America. The evening was quite an Anglo-American festive gathering. As soon as you walked up the steps you felt as though spirited back to London. The solemn so-called "controllers" of French theatres had taken themselves away for the occasion, and were not missed, while Parisians were quite surprised when a programme was actually offered to them for nothing, and no wheedling voice said, "It is thirty centimes, monsieur." That is one of the things we do better in England. The audience, being almost entirely Anglo-Saxon, was smarter in attire than a Parisian Renaissance house generally is. The ladies, however, while dressed in lighter and brighter colours than Parisiennes wear at a comedy theatre, had adopted the custom of the country in so far as they nearly all wore hats, and hats of some size, too.

If in a minority, boulevardiers were a representative minority. What did they think of *The Admirable Crichton*? Barring what is too purely and characteristically English in the dialogue to be understanded of the Parisians, the piece was one after their very hearts. They are always inclined to imagine that on our stage we must have horseplay and pranks. But here was an exquisitely slight plot without violent incidents and obvious effects, and depending for its interest on one original situation, and constantly witty dialogue. "Quite a Parisian play," I heard one Paris journalist say to another. Boulevardiers fancied the Honourable Ernest very much. Lord Loam they understood less, and looked upon wrongly as a caricature. But Crichton they thought exquisite. So beautifully English his sang-froid, his respect, and his self-respect, they pointed out to each other. And then how the Anglo-Saxon energy comes out when the party has returned to Nature, said a critic, who has read, and believes in, the French book called *What is the Cause of Anglo-Saxon Superiority?* The manners of the three aristocratic girls they considered delightful. Such peculiarly English grace, with a trifle of piquant stiffness in it, one heard them exclaim. Other characters which "fetched" the Parisians were the exquisite Lord Brocklehurst, and among the servants in the first act the French cook whom nobody thought caricatured, and the truly British groom and stable-boy. Perhaps the scene which told most effectively on the French people in the audience was that of the struggle for mastership on the island, in which Crichton, by force of nature, secures the supremacy. After the amusing procession of Lord Loam, his daughters, the Rev. John, and the Hon. Ernest, creeping slowly round the deliciously smelling pot, the curtain fell amid hearty laughter. The French spectators joined also in the merriment which greeted the scene in the hut, and the loud applause which followed the last fall of the curtain.

From the point of view of those who had already seen the play in London to-night's performance was a record one in every way. It is a literal fact that the piece never went more smoothly than this evening. The dialogue almost seemed even crisper and yet more brightly delivered than it is in London. The various situations "played" as quickly and smartly as they ever have. The stage setting was a marvel considering the pressure of time and of space also—for the resources of the Renaissance are limited—under which it was carried out. The scenery in particular of the second act, the first of the two on the island, was a great success, and some Parisian stage-managers who were present were full of admiration for the achievement. The scene was set in exactly twenty minutes. The effect of gradually on-coming dusk and night was perfectly rendered, the lights working without the suspicion of a hitch. Parisian managers averred that they had never seen a similar effect more artistically carried out on any French stage.

The fall of the act-drop upon the interior of that scene brought to Miss Irene Vanbrugh and Mr. Irving an unmistakable demonstration of popular approval. Again and again the curtain was raised, the audience applauding with great enthusiasm. The play might well have finished here. But when the curtain finally fell at the end of the fourth act occasion was taken to applaud the whole company. They have never worked so well together. The greatest triumph was certainly that of the third act, the intensity of Mr. Irving's impersonation taking the house by storm. Nothing in scenic effect was omitted, and the revolving door on the latest hotel principle, together with the punkah and the notice: "Let dogs delight to bark and bite," caused the liveliest amusement. The lighting of the beacon fires, too, caused pleasurable surprise. It was quite obvious from the undertone of observations in my neighbourhood that French people enjoyed the play, and the Cockney humour of Miss Pattie Brown and the dry unctuousness of Mr. Henry Kemble led to roars of laughter, while the reference to the little ham-and-beef shop in the Edgware Road seemed particularly the talk of the gods.

OLD HEIDELBERG

19th March, 1903

Old England is a name fraught to all of us except a few obscure national belittlers with such affectionate and sacred associations, that the title of *Old Heidelberg*, given to Mr. Bleichmann's rendering of Herr Wilhelm Meyer-Förster's patriotic German drama *Alt Heidelburg*, produced last night at the St. James's Theatre, seems to us both comprehensible and appropriate. Some reflection of the sort is, however, necessary to explain the fervour which the mention of Alt Heidelburg begets in the mind of the Teuton, to whom the name is linked with cherished memories, and is, moreover, a symbol of national pride and aspiration. First produced at the Berliner Theatre on the 22nd November, 1901, the original has enjoyed a popularity almost unrivalled on the modern German stage, has been given in the principal country theatres, and has now been seen in London and New York in German and in English. One of the first works given by the German company until lately holding possession of the Great Queen Street Theatre, it proved the most attractive in this year's repertory, and to the reception it then obtained, it is due that an adaptation has so promptly found its way on to the English stage. In reaching this something has had to be forfeited, though something also has been gained. It is improbable that in Berlin even a *mise en scène*, such as is now provided, could have been supplied. The view of the palace in Karlsburg and of the gardens in Heidelberg, with the picturesque ruins of the schloss and the haunted stream and valley of the Neckar, are things to dwell in the memory. Germany could, moreover, scarcely furnish a Prince more gallant, aristocratic, and captivating than Mr. Alexander. On the other hand, the German sentiment and passion which animate the whole and the types of German character it represents can scarcely have the same effect upon an English as upon a Teutonic audience. Be this as it may, *Alt Heidelburg* is soul-satisfying as spectacle, interesting and stirring as drama, and delectable as entertainment. It was, it is needless to say, received with the utmost enthusiasm, the curtain being lifted half a dozen times at the end of each act, and is likely to prove one of the greatest attractions of the approaching summer.

The scene of *Old Heidelberg* is, necessarily, left in Germany, and the Teutonic character of the original is scrupulously preserved. Its action oscillates between the scholars of Karlsburg, an imaginary German

Principality to which the hero is heir-apparent, and the lovely University town of Heidelberg. We see Prince Karl Heinrich tender, gentle, almost feminine, and weary of the solitary state with which he is surrounded, and listen to the preparation for his departure, and the vain attempt to thrust on his tutor and companion, Dr. Jüttner, the responsibility for making his life at Heidelberg as artificial and constrained as that he now leads. Once in the University, amid the light-hearted revelry of the students, and in the soothing presence of Käthie, the daughter of his host and the adored of all Heidelberg, Karl Heinrich unbends, while Dr. Jüttner becomes cherubic in contentment. For Käthie the Prince forms the one passion of his boyhood, and his life is sustained enchantment. The heroine is provided with a lover in Vienna. Austria is, however, a long way off, *les absents ont toujours tort*, and Käthie with interest repays her lover's passionate adoration, since even in Heidelberg Royal suitors do not grow on brambles. During four months this pleasant dream continues. It is broken by a State official who summons Karl Heinrich to Karlsburg, where his great-uncle, stricken with paralysis, is at the point of death. With a despairing and futile promise to return, he departs, and when we see him again he is a monarch immersed in State affairs, unhappier and more bored than ever, and on the point of contracting a State marriage. A casual visit of Kellermann, a faithful servant to whom in his happy days he has promised a berth, revives in him old memories and associations which flood his heart. Oblivious of all things but renascent love, he commands an immediate start for Heidelberg. Once there he meets with little but disappointment. His fellow-students, so familiar and vivacious in the presence of the Prince, have departed and their successors are cowed and ceremonious in that of the King. The entire atmosphere has changed, and there is but one person who remains the same. This is, of course, Käthie, who is roused to an ecstasy by his return, clasps him to her heart, kisses and fondles him and whispers in his ear words of rapture. All is, however, vain. She is herself on the point of getting married, and is practically as far off the King as was Charlotte from the sorrowing Werther. In an inexpressibly tender scene, accordingly, the lovers part, leaving Käthie to bear to Vienna such wifely gifts as she retains, and Karl Heinrich to resume the mill-horse round of State affairs.

A very human and familiar lesson is preached in this play, the roots of which are planted in the very depths of our nature, and the full significance of which we have not attempted to explain. It is a considerable, we might almost say a great, work, which only needs vigorous compression to enjoy almost as much vogue in England as it has experienced in Germany. For quite so much vogue it may not hope, since it depends here upon the tenderness of a love interest and the satirical sketches of Court life, and meets no demand of national sentiment. It is well treated, however, the Court scenes, even if too long, being humorous, the air of student revelry, including the drinking songs with their Latin choruses, being happily preserved, and the love passages between the Prince and his sweetheart being divinely tender. Though a mere translation, so far as may be judged the version is adequate in all respects, the mounting, as has been said, is all that can be wished, and the performance is a credit to our stage. A Karl Heinrich better than Mr. Alexander is not to be hoped, and the scenes in which he appeared delighted the audience. His appearance of youthfulness was admirably assumed, and the love scenes in which he indulged were superb. Miss Eva Moore makes a tender and gracious Käthie, who is not, of course, to be accepted merely as a sentimental heroine, but has a certain amount of undisciplined vivacity. So good a character is Dr. Jüttner that his disappearance after the early acts must be regarded as a misfortune. He was presented in finest style by Mr. J. D. Beveridge, whose reception was enthusiastic. Mr. Henry Ainley was excellent as Von Wedell, a leader among the students. Mr. E. Lyall Swete was the imposing valet, Lutz, and Mr. E. Vivian Reynolds Kellermann. So much geniality, humour, and tenderness is there in *Old Heidelberg*, that its flimsiness and its length, the latter the more serious defect, will be forgotten, and it will presumably rank among the greatest successes of the St. James's.

Pinero's *Letty*.

8th October, 1903

Letty, a play, so far as dialogue and scope go, somewhat in Mr. Pinero's earlier manner, is a difficult thing upon which to focus criticism. It leaves one, despite the keenest admiration for its art, somewhat at a loss to say precisely why the whole thing seems, on reflection, not wholly satisfying or satisfactory. Deeply interesting it is throughout; interesting for the story unfolded by its four acts and epilogue no less than for the perfect skill which construction and dialogue display. What it lacks is not the note of human probability. That is sounded clearly enough, given the characters and the circumstances which Mr. Pinero presents (Mr. Charles Frohman "presents" also, but in a less grammatical sense of the word) to our notice. What is wanting is perhaps the quality of sympathy. There is nothing sympathetic about Letchmere, Mr. Pinero's chief male character, and there is not much that is sympathetic about Letty herself. She is a clerk in a bucket-shop, who, having fallen in with an unscrupulous man-about-town, Nevill Letchmere, cherishes hopes of his responding to her great love for him by making her his wife. The first act passes in Letchmere's flat, where he entertains Letty and her friends, Marion Allardyce, a commonplace if worthy person, and Hilda Gunning, a typical "lidy" from behind a shop counter, to tea. He is interrupted in his hospitality first by a faint on Letty's part and then by a visit from Mr. Bernard Mandeville, Letty's employer. This "bounder" has at least the glimmerings of the feelings of a gentleman. His intention is to propose marriage to Letty, and he comes to warn Letchmere, whom he knows to be a married man, to "keep off the grass" and not spoil the girl's chances. To this, Letchmere, a person without scruples, coming of a stock "rotten to the core," returns a high-handed answer. After Mr. Mandeville's departure he sees the girls to a cab with a promise to join them at a humble tea-party they are giving on the roof of their lodgings, as he has "something most important" to say to Letty. This tea-party occupies the second act. It is a tolerably diverting illustration of lower middle-class vulgarity. Letchmere turns up, but his message to Letty is but one of advice to accept Mandeville's proposal when it comes, as he is a married man. On the heels of Letchmere comes the genial and

noisy bounder himself. Letty first scorns him utterly and then, broken in
health and spirit, deeply in debt, longing for the comforts which she had
hoped to share with the man she loved and of which she had tasted before
her father, a solicitor, was struck off the rolls, accepts his offer, and throws
herself into the future with a wild delirium of despair. In the next act
we see the end of one supper-party at the Café Régence and the beginning
of another. The first supper is one given by Coppinger Drake, her would-
be lover, to Mrs. Crosbie, Letchmere's sister, who, in spite of a brutal
husband, promises to be the only Letchmere to run straight. Letchmere
is devoted to her, and has promised her and himself to stick to her that
night, to ensure these final farewells ending in the lovers' parting.
Unfortunately, before he has left the room Mandeville's party, Letty
included, enter it, and he is persuaded to stay a few moments. The fun
grows fast and furious, ending in a vulgar assault on the manager by
the inebriated Mandeville. Letchmere and Letty are left alone for a
moment, and he urges her to come to him instead of attempting the
impossible in a life with this awful cad. In the fourth act she comes, and
they make somewhat half-hearted plans of travel and joy together. On
the top of this comes news that Mrs. Crosbie has bolted with Drake, and
the big scene of the play begins. The natural thing would be, one might
have thought, for Letchmere to turn upon Letty in his rage and sorrow,
and upbraid her with being the cause of his fatal desertion of his sister at
the critical moment, pointing his remarks in a way well calculated to
show Letty the kind of position to which she was resigning herself.
Mr. Pinero has not chosen this way. Instead, he makes Letchmere fly into
an ungovernable fury of sorrow rather than anger. He shouts and screams
and gulps down whisky while he shows Letty innumerable photographs
of his dainty and beloved "Tiny" at various stages of her career. The
effect is the same, however. Letty realises what it all means, what a man's
view of women may really be, and she seizes on the one moment of good
impulse in Letchmere's life to appeal to him to save one woman by letting
her go. He opens the door for her, she goes back to her lodgings, and the
big scene is at an end. That it failed to have quite the tremendous effect
evidently intended may be due to a certain amount of over-emphasis
on Mr. Irving's part, to the innate lack of sympathy with the girl's doubts
and difficulties (she is a pleasure-seeking little pig at her best), or to the
epilogue that followed. This epilogue showed Letty, two years later,
comfortably married to a smug and mean (Letty herself calls him "funny")
little photographer of the earlier scenes, bidding good-bye to Letchmere,
who turns up by chance in the Baker Street studio with Mrs. Drake,

lately Mrs. Crosbie, on his way to die at Norddrach. It is a terrible anti-climax to find that Letty should have been content to decline to so commonplace if comfortable an ending. Why Letchmere should suddenly develop consumption can be known to no one but Mr. Pinero, nor why Letty should send him away with a solemn word of "Thanks." Her saving was due entirely to accident and herself. That he let her go was due, not to any moral sense on his part, but to the force of unexpected and unusual circumstances.

There was a confusion about Letty's character that militated against sympathy. Prepared by all the earlier acts to place her as a refined girl completely out of touch with her surroundings, the shock of hearing her assert her happiness in being married to someone "of her own class" after her alliance with a hopelessly vulgar if excellent photographer was too great. The absence of teaching in the philosophy of life is, perhaps, to be deplored. But the play is one which grips attention from start to finish. It is full of wit, full of observation, and full of the laborious genius of a truly great playwright. Of the acting I must speak on another occasion. For the present, it must only be said that it was admirable throughout. Miss Irene Vanbrugh never played with greater sincerity or more consummate art. Mr. Irving made a great study of Letchmere, Miss Nancy Price scored a well-deserved triumph as the young lady from the dressmaker's, Miss Beatrice Forbes-Robertson gave an admirable sketch of the one generously human person in the play, Mr. Boucicault gave admirable expression to the delicious humours of the photographer, Mr. Fred Kerr to the vulgarities of Mandeville, while Miss Sarah Brooke, Mr. Charles Troode, and Mr. Jerrold Robertshaw were all admirably in the picture. *Letty* was received with enthusiasm. And it is, in all ways, a really notable play.

JOHN BULL'S OTHER ISLAND

1st November, 1904

For the second of his excellent series of special matinées at the Court
Theatre, Mr. J. E. Vedrenne presented yesterday afternoon for the first
time a new and unpublished play by Bernard Shaw, *John Bull's Other
Island.* If any doubts as to the genius of the author—would indeed in these
degenerate days that one might call him a playwright—exist, the fact
that he has made Irish politics a theme for the most delicious humour
imaginable will set them for ever at rest. You may care nothing in this
world for the Nationalists, the Land Purchase Act, or Home Rule, but
you will come away with your sides aching with laughter, pure natural
spontaneous merriment; and you will not find yourself asking the
question, so usual after a theatrical entertainment, "What have we been
laughing at?" You will know exactly you have laughed at the extraordinary mixture of naïveté and insouciance of the Irish race, and equally
at the delightful wrong-headedness of as typical an Englishman as was
ever put on the stage.

To tell the tale is to simply spoil the pleasure of seeing this long but
strangely fascinating piece. Strange, indeed, in another direction, for as
in human nature the tears will be very near the laughter, and you will
have the best definition of the most mystic of all religious dogmas—the
conception of the Trinity—that ever came from the Church or
Nonconformist pulpit. Strange, indeed, that there is never a jar, never a
discordant note in all this farrago. Only a genius could deal with such
a theatrical scheme. Only such a genius as Bernard Shaw could take two
snarling dogs ready to fly at each other's throats and make them romp in
a game of play. The whole piece is nearer akin to farce, geniune farce of
the Gallic pattern, but instinct with life and Gaelic humour, than anything
else in the dramatic category. It cannot be judged as a play, it is something
entirely of Bernard Shaw's own planning; but it is a delightful work all
the same; and the best of it is you can laugh at it or learn from it just as
you will. If you can do both so much the better; but there is no pointing
of the obvious moral, and none of the appeal to the cheap sentimental
moisture known as the tear.

It is Irish to the very backbone, and it has a backbone for all its curiously loose structure. Every member of Parliament may be recommended to see it; every thinking man or woman who can cram into the Court Theatre for the remaining five matinées should snatch the opportunity. To see and hear Bernard Shaw, as you can *see* him in his theatrical entertainments, is to experience a delicious refreshing draught that has the effect of straightening out a good many if not all of the tangles modern life and its stress, born of four centuries of endeavour, have woven into our web.

Barring one or two unpardonable unacquaintances with the text, the piece was played beautifully; and the fact that Mr. Granville Barker—who played an unfrocked priest and original thinker looked upon as a madman, as only an artist such as he could play it—produced it is sufficient of course to indicate the level of excellence reached. In another direction, the pleasure of stage-folk at playing in a Pinero piece is well known and understood; and anyone could see that to play in a Shaw piece means the exercise of the same fascination over its exponents. Mr. J. L. Shine as the typical Irishman who understands both points of view, the Saxon and the Celtic; Mr. Charles Daly as a parish priest, Mr. Graham Browne as a rustic as natural as the flowers of the field, Mr. A. E. George as a grim tenant farmer full of his wrongs and those of Ould Ireland, Miss Agnes Thomas as Aunt Judy, Miss Ellen O'Malley as Nora, whose heart is wrung with bitter grief, but who yet laughs at the Englishman's pronunciation of "Creina"—each and all were perfect, and there is an end of it. To pick out people for praise is merely to print the whole cast from start to finish. The two Englishmen were Mr. Louis Calvert and Mr. Nigel Playfair, and neither of them was a whit behind the excellence of the exponents from the other isle. It is a wholly delightful entertainment, over-long as it at present stands, but it would be difficult to say which of the precious lines should be sacrificed; and if the author's purpose be to show more clearly how the Irish question can be solved, then, indeed, can his triumph be added to. The "book" must surely not be allowed to remain unpublished. The description of the pig and the motor-car would make rare reading in these days of "Back to the land," "Country Notes," and "Cabbage-patch" philosophy. In the meantime let everyone who can go and enjoy *John Bull's Other Island*. It is a masterpiece, most superbly acted.

Photo: copied by Howard M. King

Nina Boucicault in "Peter Pan"

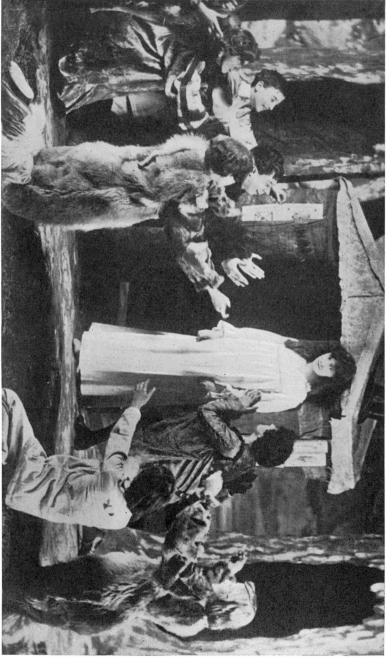

Hilda Trevelyan in "Peter Pan"

Photo: copied by Howard M. King

PETER PAN

27th December, 1904

In a spirit of delightful fancy and charming inventiveness, Mr. J. M. Barrie has conceived his Christmas story, which was last night unfolded to a crowded audience at the Duke of York's Theatre. He knows how children revel in the game of make-believe, with what elaborate care they will build up the machinery for their romances, and he has carried out the splendid idea of bringing all the resources of the stage to the service of a whimsical tale, in which sprites and pirates, Red Indians, wolves, and crocodiles, are mingled in moments of rich amusement or participate in deeds of derring-do such as Fenimore Cooper or George Henty have made familiar to the bigger boys. There is a pleasing softness, and just a tinge of sadness, about much of this story of Peter Pan, but perhaps there is a touch of too great realism when we come to the cold-blooded pirates and their dealings with the children, although Peter and his band triumph in the end, it is true, and send Captain Hook and his men to their merited doom.

Some points of Mr. Barrie's humour will be doubtless lost upon the younger members of his audiences, and even their elders may miss the meaning of a joke here and there, as for instance, when a little servant girl, a character in the play, described on the programme as its author, was sent on to "take the call" at the close last night, and to express regret that her friend, Mr. Barrie, was not in the house. These things apart, however, *Peter Pan; or The Boy Who Wouldn't Grow Up* must be pronounced an unqualified success, and one which will appeal equally to the youngsters and their parents. At a crucial moment in the story last night, it depended on the answer of the boys and girls to the pleading question, "Do you believe in fairies?" whether a certain sprite would die or not, and the unanimous affirmative showed how well the children entered into the irresponsible spirit of the entertainment. When the first baby laughed, says Mr. Barrie, that laugh broke into a thousand pieces, and every piece became a fairy, and "whenever a child says 'I don't believe in fairies,' a fairy falls down dead." In this vein of charming fancy we are carried along through some of the daintiest scenes in the play. At the outset we are introduced into a world the children will delight in. It is the Darlings' nursery, its walls friezed with animal figures and papered with pictures. And the most curious of nurses is busying herself with the evening preparations, turning on the electric light, turning down the three little beds, warming the "nighties," and preparing the bath. Nana is a great big dog, and it is Nana evidently who has frightened away certain unbidden visitors, Peter Pan and Tinker Bell. But they come again. Mr. Darling thinks Nana is becoming too important, and chains her up in the yard while he and Mrs. Darling go out to dinner. The children are tucked up in bed, when Tinker, a flickering spot of light, and Peter fly in at the window. Peter left his shadow behind on a previous visit ("There's money in that," says prosaic Mr. Darling, when it was shown to him), and now he comes to search for it. In his search he awakens Wendy Moira Angela, who, of course, isn't a bit frightened of the boy who lives "first turning to the right, and straight on till morning." When Peter was born, he ran away to the fairies rather than grow up to be a man.

He is now the captain of a band of those children who fall from perambulators, and, not being claimed in seven days, are sent to the Never Never Land. It is here that Peter takes Wendy and her two brothers, John Napoleon and Michael Nicholas, after he has taught them how to fly. The children in last night's audience laughed their heartiest when the children in the nursery were learning to trust their wings before they flew out of the window into the night. There was a reality about it all which appealed to the youngsters. The make-believe was so genuine; the stage children did not talk about flying, they flew, and right away to the Never Never Land to which Peter went after leaving the fairies. Here they find the perambulator babes grown into big boys living in the trunks of pine trees by the side of a blue lake, and Wendy plays at mothering them all and Peter plays the father, and they build Mother a house above ground "with funny little red walls and roof of mossy green." But the perambulator children must have their adventures, if only that the brave Captain Peter may come to their rescue. And so, when they are playing at families in their cosy underground home, the pirate and his band defeat the Red Indians, their friends on watch above, and carry off Wendy and the rest, who, in a fit of home-sickness, have started to journey through the forest in search of their mothers, leaving Peter behind.

But the bold, bad pirate, who is carried about in Mr. D. Jones's locker, has his own troubles. He has a hooked arm. Peter cut off the hand and threw it to a crocodile with a clock in its inside. The beast is for ever tracking the pirate captain, but he can always hear it coming by the sound of the internal tick-tick. As one of his faithful band reminds him, some day the clock will run down, and then the crocodile will have him. We will not tell how Peter rescues the children from as cruel-looking a pirate ship as ever sailed the Spanish Main, or by what ruse it is that he is able, after leading his band in a hotly contested fight with Captain Hook and his crew, to lower the skull and crossbones and hoist the Union Jack to the strains of *Rule Britannia*. All this is duly set forth by Mr. Barrie, who brings Wendy and her brothers back to the nursery none too soon, for their mother is pining for them, and their father, in his remorse, has taken to living in the dog-kennel. *Peter Pan* is delightfully acted. Miss Nina Boucicault is brave and charming as Peter, and Miss Hilda Trevelyan makes of Wendy a most engaging little mother, her two brothers being capitally represented by Master George Hersee and Miss Winifred Geoghegan. Miss Dorothea Baird makes a welcome return to the stage in the character of the real mother, and as the real father and the pirate king Mr. Gerald du Maurier embodies the dual rôle with unfailing skill. His pirate king, with his expurgated oaths and melodramatic airs, is a splendid piece of burlesque. Warm praise is also due to Messrs. George Shelton and Sydney Harcourt as a couple of pirates, and to Mr. Arthur Lupino for making such a lovely dog and helping so much towards the enthusiastic success of Mr. Barrie's children's play.

SARAH'S HAMLET

Sarah's Hamlet. First let us see what a fine rhapsodist had to say about Sarah's genius in general. In *Punch and Judy* Maurice Baring wrote:

I believe that the secret of her art was that of all great art: that she was guided by an infallible instinct, and that whatever she did she could not go wrong. When what she did was done, it seemed simple, inevitable, and easy; and so swiftly accomplished, that you had no time to think of the *how*; nor was your sense sharp enough, however carefully you watched, to detect the divine conjury. It was the same whether she spoke lines of La Fontaine and Racine, or whether she asked, as she poured out a cup of coffee, as she did in one play: "*Du sucre, deux morceaux?*" She was artistically inerrant. It is this gift which was probably the secret of the great actors of the past: Garrick, Siddons, Talma, and Salvini. It is certainly to be seen in the work of the great singer of the present, Chaliapine, whether he is portraying Satan holding his court on the Brocken, or a foolish, good-natured Chinovnik, half-fuddled with drink after a night out. When such a gift is at work, the greater the material it is interpreting, the greater, of course, the effect.

The greater the play Sarah Bernhardt appeared in, the greater the demand on her instinct, which *was* her genius; the swifter and the fuller the response. As the occasion expanded, so did her genius rise to it.

Her Hamlet was and is still hotly discussed, and quite lately several eminent English writers have expressed opinions that are completely at variance with one another on the subject. But every critic when he reads *Hamlet* creates a Hamlet in his own image, and when he sees it acted, the more vivid the impersonation, the more likely it is to be at variance with his own conception. One critic finds her Hamlet an unpardonable Gallic liberty to take with Shakespeare; another, that she electrified Hamlet with the vigour of her personality. I remember a cultivated philosopher, who was a citizen of the world, telling me that he thought her Hamlet the only intelligible rendering he had seen of the part, just because it rendered the youthful inconsequence of the moods of the moody Dane. But whether you thought it justifiable or unjustifiable, true or untrue to Shakespeare, in witnessing it you were aware of the genius of the interpreter answering the genius of the dramatic poet. Deep was calling to deep.

When Hamlet looked into the guilty King's face at the end of the play within the play, or thought for one second that the King and not Polonius had blundered into death behind the arras; when Hamlet concealed his forebodings from Horatio, and when Hamlet looked at Laertes during the duel and let him know that he knew the swords had been exchanged and that one of them had been poisoned, all thought of the part—the rendering, tradition, the language, the authorship went to the winds: you knew only that something which had been invented by one great genius was being interpreted by another great genius, and that the situation had found an expression which was on its own level.

But then Maurice, like some other critics, was perhaps not quite sane on the subject of Sarah. Here, out of its envelope, is a calmer estimate of what must still have been an extraordinary performance:

4th April, 1905

The appearance at the Adelphi of Mdme. Bernhardt as Hamlet has been, so far at least as fashionable London is concerned, the theatrical event of the season. In Paris the performance was received with unequivocal raptures, and there are many who hold it to be the greatest triumph in a career made up of triumphs. In London the interest is that chiefly of curiosity and admiration for the actress. In this aspect, even, some deduction has to be made. By appearing a couple of years ago as Lorenzaccio Mdme. Bernhardt showed us what we were to expect in Hamlet, and the conclusions deduced from that performance prove in almost every respect to be accurate. Not very ready were we in early days to accept a French Hamlet, though the success of Fechter, to mention none other, removed some illusions. There are, indeed, still living some who hold Fechter's Hamlet the most interesting the world has seen. If we accept Hamlet as the typical *jeune premier*, earnest, impassioned, amorous, gallant and picturesque, it satisfied most requirements. Female Hamlets, meanwhile, whether the exponent be named Cushman, Marriott, or what not, are, and always will be, a delusion and a snare. For a Frenchwoman to play Hamlet before an English public is an experiment daring and unique. Mdme. Bernhardt is not the first female Hamlet that has been seen in France, Mdme. Judith, a relative of Rachel, having taken the rôle in an adaptation of the play by her husband, Bernard-Dérosne. This, however, did not appeal to English suffrages. It may at once be said that the Hamlet now exhibited will win no acceptance from English scholars. Society will, no doubt, rave about it, and there is much about which to rave. If Hamlet were other than he is we might praise the beauty, grace, and finesse of the rendering. Hamlet is, however, something other than a brisk, picturesque, vivacious, and amorous stripling, who dismisses sorrow with a gibe, and overflows with animal spirits.

It is, perhaps, no longer expedient to dwell in a newspaper report upon what Hamlet is. It may, however, and must be said that he is all Mdme. Bernhardt is not. In appearance, Mdme. Bernhardt is graceful. No question arises concerning Hamlet being fat or scant of breath. With her fair hair clustering round her head, a short tunic, apparently of black silk trimmed with sable, black hose, and a long and flowing silk cloak, she is the ideal of a young prince, whose sorrows, even if fantastical, are at least vivaciously and effectively expressed. The "antic" disposition Hamlet elects to exhibit accounts for some impertinences of conduct, such as thrusting into the face of the King the torch which has been seized during the play scene. There is much of this class in the performance that is ingenious and little that is indefensible. What we miss is the burden which Hamlet strives to bear, and under which he sinks. Occasionally, as in the scene in which he climbs almost on to the raised throne of the King, when the monarch is "frighted with false fire," Hamlet is too demonstrative. As a rule his gestures are few and significant, and there is a wholly to be commended absence of all strain after effect. The version in which Mdme. Bernhardt appears is a genuine rendering and is, it may be assumed, the most faithful ever put upon the French stage. All the things against which Voltaire and the Academy protested, and which, in the height of the movement of romanticism, Dumas dared not retain, are preserved, and there are moments when English freedom, apt to be a little shamefaced, is surpassed.

All the wonders of the original are accomplished, the naïve and not too decent songs of Ophelia, banished from the version in which Mdme. Bernhardt previously appeared, herself playing Ophelia, are restored; and the utterances of the gravediggers are stripped of none of their grotesqueness, and prove in French hands sufficiently diverting. All the liberty that has been taken consists of omissions and abbreviations pardonable enough in any case, and indispensable in that of a play so long as *Hamlet*. When many scenes had been abridged, and some entirely excised, the play lasted over four hours, a time too long for a London public. In justice to the management it should be said that the waits, though numerous, were in no case long, and that the business was rattled through in a style not common on similar occasions. The scene of most importance that entirely disappeared was that in which Laertes takes his farewell of his father and sister, and he and Polonius both lecture Ophelia on the manner in which she should treat the advances of Hamlet. Many of the scenes were well managed; the ghost effects were effective, and the manner in which in the chamber scene the apparition of the murdered King walked, so to speak, out of his portrait on the wall, was to be commended. Less good was the disposition of the play scene, the King and Queen being too far removed from Hamlet. The address to the players was spoken by Hamlet while a valet was lighting the footlights of the mimic representation, and a small orchestra with flutes and recorders was seated in front of the false stage. During the play scene the manner of Hamlet to Ophelia was caressing and amorous. He all but sat as he proposes on her lap, and he pressed endearingly with his hand her fair head.

On these things there is no temptation to dwell. Every point that can be made in the rendering of *Hamlet* has been tried, and every accessory that can simplify action has been adopted. We are, indeed, a little wearied of forced points and impossible readings. Mdme. Bernhardt affords us no revelation or illumination. No woman has done this, and none ever will. The more inspired and divine a woman is, the less fitted is she to play Hamlet. There is, however, no need to treat the new Hamlet with ungracious coldness or discouragement. Mdme. Bernhardt gives us conspicuous proof of courage and capacity, and does all that can be done to achieve the impossible. Her Hamlet is more than inoffensive. It is always bright and attractive, often impressive, and sometimes suggestive. Mdme. Bernhardt was received with rapture, the calls of the audience were too numerous to be counted, and the entertainment, so far as society is concerned, is a prodigious success. All the afternoon and evening representations that can be given are too few to meet the exigencies of the British public, and some at least of those most anxious to see the performance will be unable to do so. The general cast was moderate, but not specially striking. The Ophelia was the typical French *ingénue*. The gravediggers were really diverting.

IRVING'S LAST DAYS

Irving's Last London Appearance.

29th April, 1905

The fears concerning his short London season, inspired by the illness which interrupted Sir Henry Irving's country tour, proved happily groundless and the great actor appeared duly on Saturday night in the promised revival of *Becket.* The occasion was well calculated to inspire enthusiasm, and the great and friendly audience, consisting, as heretofore, of those most noteworthy in the world of art, society, and literature, greeted Sir Henry with rapture, which, in the case of one less highly endowed, might be regarded as extravagant. In these the note of relief was no less assertive than that of affection, and the joy of having among us once more the creator of so many masterpieces was overpoweringly manifest. It is, perhaps, impossible to say that the character of Becket as conceived by Tennyson is the greatest in which the actor has been seen. Memories of Matthias, Louis XI, and a dozen other parts, down to Corporal Gregory Brewster, rise up to check such pronouncement. It may, however, be declared the most imaginative and poetical that Sir Henry, or any other actor, has given us for many a year. No inducement exists to open out fresh disputes, natural and appropriate enough when first stirred, as to Sir Henry's conception of the Cardinal, which shows him saint and martyr, rather than an active and fairly aggressive ecclesiastic, and leaves behind an impression of piety rather than power. So completely did the Irving conception prevail for stage purposes that it is little likely that another will be presented, and certain that, whose it is, it will not be tolerated.

The present rendering is virtually indistinguishable from the first. It is a little mellower, perhaps, in tone, but is no less fixed in steadfastness and radiant in devotion. But few opportunities are afforded us of seeing the priest as the King's friend and ally, and the short scene over the chessboard seems to us to have been abridged. When we come to Northampton the change of nature in the prelate is accomplished, the friend is sunk in the priest, and the *non possumus,* to which so loyally and constantly, and

Photo: copied by Howard M. King

Cissie Loftus and Hilda Trevelyan in "Peter Pan"

Photo: Rigal, Paris

Jeanne Granier in "La Petite Mariée"

Photo: W. and D. Downey

Connie Gilchrist

Photo: S. A. Walker

Florence St. John

with so fatal effect, the Archbishop adheres, has been pronounced. A species of climax is reached when, in Northampton Hall, Becket defies menace and repels entreaty, and in so doing effects his first breach with the King. For the scenes in or near Rosamund's bower, we have never greatly cared. Rosamund de Clifford herself will always remain a tender and touching personage, and the scenes between her and the offended Queen are enshrined in history and consecrated in legend. If they seem melo-dramatic in action and suggestive of the "penny plain twopence coloured" style of illustration, no one is really to blame. A sort of self-consciousness begotten of burlesque asserts its sway, and no responsibility belongs to author or actor. A distinct loss to dignity, not at all redeemed by a species of conventional prettiness, attends the bringing on of the Archbishop as protector and councillor, and, if need be, saviour of this Royal mistress. That such an assumption is historically untrue does not matter in the least; it detracts, however, from the impressive dignity of the central figure, and is almost to be branded as a catchpenny invention. The scenes in the fourth act—accepting the first as a prologue—remain beautiful and dramatic, the figure of the Cardinal towers into sublimity, and the death scene is intense, dramatic, and almost, if not quite, tragic. There would be no question of its being less than tragic if the motive of Becket's opposition to the King, and his entire change of front in things ecclesiastical, were a little less nebulous.

From the moment when Sir Henry Irving came on the stage his triumph was assured. Such a shout of approval as rang through the house has seldom been heard in a theatre, and some moments had to elapse before the *partie* at chess, between monarch and prelate, could be continued. The same frenzied welcome attended the Archbishop throughout, and there was not a scene in which Becket appeared that did not bring down shouts of acclamation. Strangely stirring was the reception of the priest at the close of the first act; while the acting in the fourth act elicited clamour of applause. The picturesque poetical figure stirred one as before, the delivery was only less limpid than it previously was, and the influence of much touring in the English counties and America was scarcely to be felt.

So far as our memory serves, none of the original cast reappear. Miss Ellen Terry was, of course, the Rosamund. Her place is now taken by Miss Maud Fealy, who certainly deserves the appellation of fair, usually coupled with Rosamund, since she is blonde enough for a Viking's bride. Mr. Gerald Lawrence takes the part of the King, played in remarkable style by Mr. William Terriss, and is not less regal, impulsive, and impetuous than his predecessor. Mrs. Cecil Raleigh, replacing Miss Genevieve Ward, obtained a great success as the imperious and tragic Queen. Miss Grace Hampton was Margery. The general presentation by actors, many of them unknown to London, was creditable and commendable. The reappearance of Sir Henry in our midst assigns the season the requisite sense of fitness, and invests it with a dignity previous seasons have missed. It is a delight to witness our great actor in strength and vigour unimpaired, and to think that London will have a further chance of seeing him in a series of his greatest parts. The unfortunate destruction a few years ago of his scenery will, we fancy, alone prevent him from entering into the fray, and disputing for the supremacy in *Hamlet*, which seems to be the object of the season's competition. A cruel and ill-judged insistence on the part of the audience for a speech, elicited only a few words of acknowledgment and thanks.

ELLEN TERRY'S JUBILEE

I saw Ellen Terry in *Alice-Sit-By-The-Fire* at the Gaiety Theatre, Manchester, on the evening following Irving's death. At the words "It's summer done, autumn begun. Farewell, summer, we don't know you any more. Alice Sit-by-the-fire henceforth. Taxis farewell—advance four-wheelers. I had a beautiful husband once, black as the raven was his hair . . ." she broke down, the curtain was lowered, and the audience filed out without a sound. "He looked like some beautiful grey tree that I have seen in Savannah" she had written a few months before.

The last of the Envelopes deals with Ellen Terry's Jubilee, which took place in 1906.

In dealing with the Ellen Terry Jubilee matinée of yesterday at Drury Lane the evening papers had up to a point the best of it. Since then the morning papers have had their more leisured say, and the speeches which were delivered late in the afternoon have doubtless been widely reported. But a good deal came between the performance of the first act of *Much Ado* and the "reception" with which, towards six, the proceedings were brought to a close. Mlle. Adeline Genée and Mr. P. Sundberg danced a *pas de deux;* Signor Caruso, "down" for a song, had to give two; and Miss Ellaline Terriss made a second appearance. She had already posed as Cinderella in the tableau reproducing Millais's picture, the original sitter for which was, we believe, Miss Lucy Buckstone, daughter of J. B. Buckstone, the famous comedian. This time it was Miss Terriss's fate to sing of the "lots of things you never learn at school," and with her reappeared the Bath Buns. Then came a "Minstrel Entertainment" which, with Mr. Seymour Hicks in charge, proved one of the most exhilarating items of the bill. The strength of the minstrel company may be gauged by the fact that Mr. Willie Edouin was among the "bones," and Mr. Edmund Payne among the "tambourines"! Then Miss Gertie Millar having sung "In Rotterdam" and Mr. Lewis Waller having delivered Henry V's speech at the siege of Harfleur, came the last, and best, scene of all. Standing alone before a flame-coloured curtain, which, as we afterwards learnt, concealed Miss Ellen Terry and a crowd of eminent people connected with the stage, Lady Bancroft addressed a few words to the audience, words that were wise, heartfelt, and unaffected. Her delivery was a lesson. Drury Lane is a very exacting house, and Lady Bancroft did not seem to make any exertion. She spoke simply and quietly, but every word was heard. She disclaimed all intention of making, or rather of reading, a set speech, and just said what she felt. And she evidently felt a great deal as she expressed her gratification that this was not a farewell, and touched on what a farewell appearance means to an artist who has lived for many years on the public's applause. She would not wish *Sweet Nell of Old Drury* another fifty years, that would be a rather "large order"; but she hoped it would be long ere Miss Terry and the public parted company. It was the point at which the curtain should rise, and Lady Bancroft, while expressing doubt as to her being taken to be a fairy and obeyed, gave the signal. The curtain rose. On a raised throne in the middle sat Miss Ellen Terry, clad in white and looking as young and charming as when she appeared as Beatrice. On the view the wishing her another fifty years was not so absurd after all. Miss Terry, who was surrounded by her family, by her friends, by everybody, quickly descended from her throne, and, taking Lady Bancroft's hand, kissed it. Then, with a voice trembling with emotion, she spoke as follows:

My dear Lady Bancroft—my friend of many years—my kind manager of sweet, old days—how can I thank you? You greet me last to make the end more sweet.

Never have I felt so strongly as now that language was given me, at any rate, to conceal rather than to reveal. I have no words at all to say what is in my heart—indeed, I don't realise what *is* in my heart— and I can only trust to my friends on the stage and in the audience to be eloquent for me.

If I began to thank every one who has had a share in making this day so wonderful for me, I should never be able to stop. There is Mr. Collins, who has lent this great theatre with its inspiring memories. There is the Committee who, with their Chairman at their head, and their faithful Secretary always to hand, have done all that men can do, and more, to make the wheels go round. There are the gentlemen of the Press whose work for the success of this afternoon has been of the greatest value to the Committee and to me. There are my brothers and sisters in art who first inspired this performance, and have since been the very head and front of it. There are my foreign comrades who have joined with those of my own country in the celebration of my Jubilee:

to each and all I owe a debt of gratitude, which must always remain unpaid. I have the *heart* to wonder at all that you have done for me, but not the tongue to praise you.

I will not say good-bye. It is one of my chief joys to-day that I need not say good-bye—just yet, but can still say I am on the active list—still one of *you*—(turning to people on stage) —and still *your* servant—(to audience)—if you please !

The "old sweet days" were at the Prince of Wales's, where Miss Ellen Terry first played Portia, to the Shylock of Mr. Coghlan. When she came to speak of the foreign artists she indicated Signor Caruso, and taking the hand of Signora Duse, bowed, and kissed it. Signora Duse clasped Miss Terry in her arms. When Miss Terry had finished, Mr. Pinero, stepping out of the crowd on the stage, stated that the matinée had realised close on £6,000, which is £1,000 in excess of the sum realised at Nellie Farren's benefit. Thanks, indirectly, to the London County Council, the "capacity" of the theatre has recently been increased. The curtain fell. But it had to rise several times yet. The last glimpse of Miss Ellen Terry was as one of an interlaced, happy group of three, the others being Miss Kate Terry and Miss Marion Terry. The audience sang "Auld Lang Syne" just as it did at Sir Henry Irving's final appearance at the same theatre just a year ago. Miss Terry departed to face another ovation in the evening, when she appeared as Lady Cicely Waynfleet in *Captain Brassbound's Conversion* at the Court. The audience dispersed slowly. The jaded pittites blinked as they emerged into daylight and bought evening papers that they might read about it all before going to bed.

It is fitting that this book which begins with Irving should end with Ellen Terry. I am indebted to our exquisite film-critic for the glittering remark that the written word cannot bring the dead to life again. Be it so. May I hope that the dramatic critics whom I have cited have left something to remind the modern theatre-goer that in an older day such players were.